Take Me Back

CHARLES B NEELY

Copyright © 2012 Charles B Neely
All rights reserved.

ISBN: 1466477407
ISBN 13: 9781466477407

Library of Congress Control Number: 2011919568
CreateSpace, North Charleston, SC

Proclamations, Disclaimers, & other & sundry denials of wrongdoing

If you are reading this then lets assume you are about to read the stories that follow. In them, the characters quite often seem to have left their halos' at home. If this offends you I am not in the least bit sorry. Each of us must follow his own conscience and anyway all things change with the inexorable passage of time.

All of the events and people named in this book are real. Memory being a somewhat fallible source of data, the people involved may have a differing recollection of details, or their own role in the story, but all I can say to that is write your own darn book then.

Lastly, and possibly most importantly, if there is anything written in this book that could be used in a prosecutorial manner, or in any way points the finger of illegality at any person, it is a lie…… or maybe I just misremembered.

Hope you enjoy the book!

    Buck Neely
    July 6 2011
    Moon Lake, Mississippi

Foreward

On the surface, the stories in *Take Me Back* might appear to be a collection of whimsical remembrances of a young boy growing into a true hunter-man, however, if one steps back one can find more than just mere stories, but also a treasure trove of life lessons as well as a "How To Hunt Birds" manual. Buck's attention to detail in his pictorial description catapults the reader directly into the middle of the bygone scene. I found myself smiling with pride at his first kill, and giggling at some of the innocent excitement and complete abandon of Buck's early activities at the various hunting locations, and full out belly laughing at some of the mischievous predicaments Buck and his friends found themselves into.

    Not being a hunter myself the specific hunting and gun jargon was unfamiliar, however, the picture he painted helped me fill in my own version of a gun or hunting scene that I thought would be proper. To the hunting sage who knows all about the seasons, the guns, the birds, well this book is like a walk through a candy store where one can almost taste each delicious morsel retrieving distinct memories of their own early hunting days.

Delicately interspersed within the fascination lies deep wisdom about hunting all kinds of birds. Nash Buckingham himself, a most revered hunter, author, storyteller lends his very own wisdom on hunting doves. Nuggets of hunter savvy are sprinkled within the pages of *Take Me Back*. The reader will discover things like what different weather patterns mean to the success of the day's hunt in one sentence, and then find first rate hunter safety information in the very next.

It's obvious that the author, Buck Neely's childhood was rich in opportunities of a rare and unique nature. The quirky (and highly intelligent) inquisitiveness of his parents allowed Buck to see life and nature in a way few others have. *Take Me Back* is written with the penchant directly resulting from the varied learning and life experiences Buck knew on a daily basis.

Take Me Back will be one of the most read books at any hunting camp. However it also reads well with a snifter of brandy beside the crackling fire at home, or by the small illumination of a flashlight snuggled under the comforter of a warm bed on the eve of any hunting season. Imparting wisdom, virtues, ethics, and humor, *Take Me Back* appeals to any aged hunter, or want-to-be hunter, and will be revisited season after season after season.

Written by:
Clare Patton
Spokane, Washington
10/21/11

A special thanks to Therese Albury, of Man-O-War Cay, Abaco, Bahamas. She did my proof reading, and it was embarrassing. If you find any errors it is just southern vernacular, or it is her fault. Thanks Therese.

Contents

1:	Summer Job	1
2:	Pick-up Man	13
3:	Training Days	25
4:	Mistletoe	41
5:	Hatchie Coon Rules	45
6:	"Ole Reliable"	57
7:	The Truman Blind	67
8:	The Bayou	79
9:	Steele	87
10:	Heroes and Outlaws	97
11:	Mallard Hole	107
12:	Bait	121
13:	Indiana Ray	129
14:	Old ways	137
15:	Mentors and Ethics	143

Summer Job

When mom put breakfast on the table it was still dark outside. I had already fed Francis (the pig) and still had the chickens to do, but that would have to be after breakfast because some of what they would get, we were working on first: over-easy eggs with the edges crispy because that's the way they come out of a black-iron skillet; a piece of super-salty home made country ham; red-eye gravy and cantaloupe from the garden. Mom would never spend any money on "fruit loops" or "coco-puffs" like my friends got to eat but that was ok, I like salt. I hurried up because Unkoo would be here shortly and I was going with him "out to the farm" which I did several times a week during the summer. I was a worker. It was my job to open gates. I was seven years old.

It was already "sticky" outside as it usually is in Memphis, Tennessee in June. I put a half-bucket of scratch grain under the big pine in back of the house and the cantaloupe rinds, which had a good rim of fruit left on them. It would be completely picked clean in a few hours. The chickens we had were half Bantam and half Buckingham round-heads, and they were mean. That last half was a breed of fighting cocks that my grandfather developed and we crossed them with Bantams so that they could fly well enough to get away from the neighbors' dogs. They were wild as a deer, could fly like a pigeon, and fight like it was for money.

I put the food out and scampered out of the way. There were too many roosters and they didn't like me nor I them. Mom said we were going to make fried chicken out of most of them and that I could help with my BB gun. I was looking forward to it. I had been practicing on blue jays for quite some time and they were getting pretty scarce. Unkoo told me that blue jays knock the other bird's eggs out of the nest and lay their own there. I never could stand a bully. He also put a twenty-five cent bounty on every one I could get. I had money and a purpose, what more could one ask for?

I need to explain something here that might not be immediately apparent. We lived in the middle of town. The fact that we kept chickens, goats, pigs, emus, alligators, etc., seemed quite natural to me at the time, but we did live in the middle of a large city. It was a big yard, and the neighbors had big yards with lots of big oak trees and we had a fence... eventually, but the chickens didn't respect property lines. The only complaint we ever got was just a comment or two about the crowing, which I took care of. Our maid, Martha, was the best fried-chicken cook ever!

I was waiting on the front porch when Unkoo turned in our driveway. He was a medium sized man, stocky, short arms, dark hair cut short, habitual khakis with straw cowboy hat in summer, and boots. His grin was infectious and he had a humorous disposition with a dose of the practical joker. He was my mother's brother, Hugh L. Buckingham, my outdoors mentor, and I loved him like a father.

"Get in Monster" he said, "we've got stops to make before we get out of town."

The first of these was Mr. Jimmy's Three Little Pigs Barbeque on Highland Street. Mr. Jimmy had a box of pork skins with fat still on them for the dogs. Unkoo kept a kennel with some very fine bird dogs in it, which, in accordance with the times, were English setters and he believed in fat for their coats. I liked chewing on the skins also and mom said my hair was always greasy so I guess it worked. Next was a parts store- something for a tractor- and finally the obligatory Germantown coffee club, which was held in the back of the hardware store off Poplar Avenue. My job, during all this, was to be quiet, carry stuff, and say "yes sir" when spoken to. I was good at it.

Eventually we arrived out at the farm, swapped the grey car with it's plastic covered back seat and hangover gun racks, for a blue truck, step-side as trucks were in 1967, also with gun racks, only these were mounted across the back window. The kennels were dirty, and Big Jim, one of several colored men who lived on the place got a "talking to" from my usually jovial uncle. I slipped off and fed pork skins to my two favorites, Queenie and Suzy.

Next we checked cows. I rode in the back, straddling the side and facing forward, like in a rodeo. One leg was inside the bed and the other rested on top of the fender. With my fingers wrapped under the curled up edge of the truck bed, I couldn't be thrown off. As soon as we pulled up to a gate I would hit the ground running, open up, close behind, and back in the saddle as fast as possible. Unkoo said "cows can smell an open gate," so we never left any open.

Around noon it was our norm to end up at the cabin. Cold cuts with white bread, pickles and tomatoes made up our fare with sweet tea and iron-water ice cubes, from the old metal ice trays with the lever on top, and dumped into the green sweaty ice bucket.

Unkoo liked a "siesta" out in the hammock under the two ancient cedars after lunch. Like most young boys, I had to keep moving, and besides, there was a three acre bass lake in the pasture right next to the cabin. I decided to go fishing.

There were two rods hanging on pegs over the fireplace in the cabin. One, a spinning rod with twenty pound test line had been my companion for quite some time and it had caught many a green-backed bass from the muddy, cattle-stained waters about. I took down the other rod with some trepidation. It was a bait-casting model, also with twenty pound test, which is apparently the breaking strength deemed necessary to withstand the rigors of a seven year old. My proficiency with this weapon was by no means certain but I had been told that mastery of said equipment was a prerequisite for other types of fishing that my uncle engaged in, namely tarpon. If I wanted to get invited to go, I had to learn.

Knots were also deemed important knowledge. I could tie a clinch knot, a granny, and sometimes a spider-hitch (all prerequisites for tarpon fishing) but sometimes my knots didn't look that great. Inspection revealed that a two bladed spinner, yellow and black, was already on the rod and somebody far neater than I had put it there. Perfect, if it ain't broke don't fix it!

Skinny is good for squeezing through a rail fence and I was soon stalking up to the shallow end of the lake. Standing back from the edge helps to keep from spooking bass that like to hide right up under the grass, and it also helps to keep my bare legs a little further from the most likely resting places of the numerous cotton-mouths of the area.

I set the tension knob with the reel in free-spool, as per instruction, and got ready to heave. With the grass so tall, I had to get it going in a long side arm type motion, and, remembering to thumb, let her rip.

Thirty minutes later, while I was back on the porch and still picking and plucking at the biggest backlash mankind has ever seen, Unkoo gets out his pocketknife and cuts all the line from the reel. I held the spool and he wound on the new. "Good as new Monster, all you need is an educated thumb. Keep practicing and don't get discouraged, you'll get it." I didn't think so.

An inherently intuitive uncle, he immediately set up a new quest. "I promised Callie some bream," he says, " and I need you to help me catch some." It is amazing how fast a little boy can go from the depths of despair to the pinnacle of enthusiasm.

Callie was cook for my granddad and Unkoo. Large, black, robust and ageless, she was of the upper point one percentile for kindness in the human race and especially to little boys. She had a tendency to always have cakes, pies, or cookies stashed away from the mainstream household but available from the kitchen door, away from any parental disapproval. If she wanted brim, I was going to make sure she got a big mess of them!

We loaded two cane poles, a wire fish basket and a cricket cage into the back of the truck and headed towards "Brim's Lake" at the back of the farm. It was in an area known as "the bottom" because the hills dropped off into the flood plane of Nonconna Creek. A levee had been erected across one of the draws leading into the bottom, and run-off from the pastureland kept the lake full. It also washed nutrients into the lake and grew some of the biggest, fattest, blue-gilled brim in Tennessee.

We parked at the end of the levee and walked down a ways to where a fence post stuck out of the water about fifteen feet from the bank. In the vicinity of this post, but under water, were round coils of barbed wire and pea-gravel for the brim to nest in. This man made brim bed worked like a charm for many years and drastically reduced the amount of effort required to find the fish.

I carried the cane poles and the crickets. I had helped make the poles and these were not just thrown together rigs. A proper cane pole has the line, clear mono about ten to twelve pound test, tied to the middle of the pole and wound around in a spiral all the way to the tip, where it is again tied off. The reason for this is that a jumbo catfish or lunker bass will occasionally feast on your cricket and the ensuing battle might break your pole. This way, you at least have a chance to drag, or hand-line the fish to the bank. The line should be no longer than 4/5 the length of the pole, for stand-up use, and ¾ the length for sitting. This aids in a controlled swing and accurate bait placement. The cork is made from a porcupine quill for the utmost sensitivity and a tiny split shot, three inches above a long shanked cricket hook rounds out the equipment. For just brim, we used the light wire hooks, but if bigger fish were expected the stouter hooks were the norm.

Next, a cricket is impaled from the head to rear, or rear to head, but at any rate lengthwise. When you grab a cricket, whatever hold you get is what you keep- don't try to shift or you will lose a lot of crickets.

We were ready to fish.

Unkoo took up his usual station on a convenient old stump. I, being young and fidgety, moved up and down the bank.

Bait up, swing out, pause, twitch it, pick up and try a new spot. "Brim like an active bait," he tells me, "and if they don't take it right off, move it- even a few inches will make a difference."

We caught brim. Big orange- breasted males that I couldn't put my little hand around and that peed a stream two feet out when grabbed for de-hooking. One spot would produce five or six fish as fast as you could get a bait to them and then you had to prospect around a few feet and find another producing spot. Most of the time a brim will just twitch the quill, or jerk it straight down. If the quill moves slow-steady, and at a slant, there's a good chance it is a big bass or catfish. In this case don't jerk too hard; you might break your pole.

"Brim are the fight-in-est fish in fresh water, pound for pound," Unkoo said, "and on these big ones, as with any big fish, you got to play-em. Let the pole do the work and tire 'em out first." I wasn't much on playing them. My cork went under and I yanked back with everything I had, the line going in tight circles the way brim do, until the fish lost traction when it broke the surface and went flying in an ark over my head to slam in the dust behind me. It was fairly effective.

In a couple of hours we had enough brim for both families, and plenty for gifting. I was chasing the last cricket around in the cage while Unkoo started to pack up. I had him, but he got loose and started up my arm. His next jump put him almost in the grass but a quick pounce and he was mine. Through the chest and out the rear, my favorite way, and I swung him all the way out past the post and into deep water. The split shot slowly pulled the cricket under- he was a big, fat cricket with lots of buoyancy- and the quill slowly started to right itself. Before getting completely vertical, it paused, changed direction, and began moving off on a parallel course to the bank. I yanked back with my tried and true flip-over-the-head technique but this was different, the fish just kept right on going as if nothing was wrong and I had no choice but to follow. Within a few yards the tempo picked up and I was running, luckily still down the bank, and holding on for dear life. Nearing the end of the levee, the fish finally decided he wanted freedom, and came out of the water in a long head-shaking tail walk. I heard Unkoo give a rebel yell from the truck but I was too busy to look up. As if the yell were a signal, this enormous fish that we now knew was a bass of gargantuan proportions, turned away from the bank taking me with him. The water was shallow here, but the mud was deep. Both of my tennis shoes, that mom bought two sizes too big so I could grow into them, came off immediately which was a big help. My uncle was running up and down the bank yelling well intentioned but conflicting instructions: "Don't horse him! Don't horse him! Easy-Easy! Put some pressure on him-don't horse him! Turn his head toward the bank... Easy...Easy." By then I was in waist-deep water and turning the fish was fast becoming a necessity of the first order. I found that I could lead him around in circles with a steady cane-pole-creaking-line-twanging side-pull, but if I let off for a second he pulled me into ever deepening water, and I was already loosing traction. When he jumped again I saw it coming and leaned out towards him as far as I could. Luckily, line and hook held and after the following surge I was able to gain a few feet back toward the bank. The water was a bit shallower here and he didn't like it- we were at a standoff. About then I heard some splashing and Unkoo was at my side and he had a dip-net. "Just lead him back and forth easy, and I'll try to intercept him when he comes by." The fish dodged the net on the first pass, with a big splash, and my heart sank because I thought he had gotten off. On the second pass I was able to pull him to the surface for a moment, Unkoo leaned out, the fish lunged, there was a loud "snap!" as the line parted, and I went over backwards.

When I came up, sputtering, Unkoo had the bass in the net, water was flying everywhere, and he had the biggest grin on his face I had ever seen; maybe as big as the one on my own face.

Later that afternoon, after we had weighed the fish at Bub Ross's country store, Buck Patton, the sports writer for the Memphis paper, showed up at the farm to take a picture for the Sunday paper. The faded old clipping of forty-three years past, shows a grinning, blond haired, toothpick legged, sunburned boy, bending over a washtub and trying to hold up an enormous large-mouthed bass. The caption reads "Buck Neely, nephew of Hugh L. Buckingham, with a bass caught at the Buckingham Plantation this past week. Weight: 10 and ½ lbs."

Since that day, probably more than half a lifetime ago, I have caught some big fish: Tarpon in Mexico, Tuna and Amberjack in the Gulf, Salmon in Alaska and jumbo catfish in the Mississippi River. None of these ever gave me the thrill of that farm-pond bass. Come to think of it, I don't think I ever had a better day "at work" either.

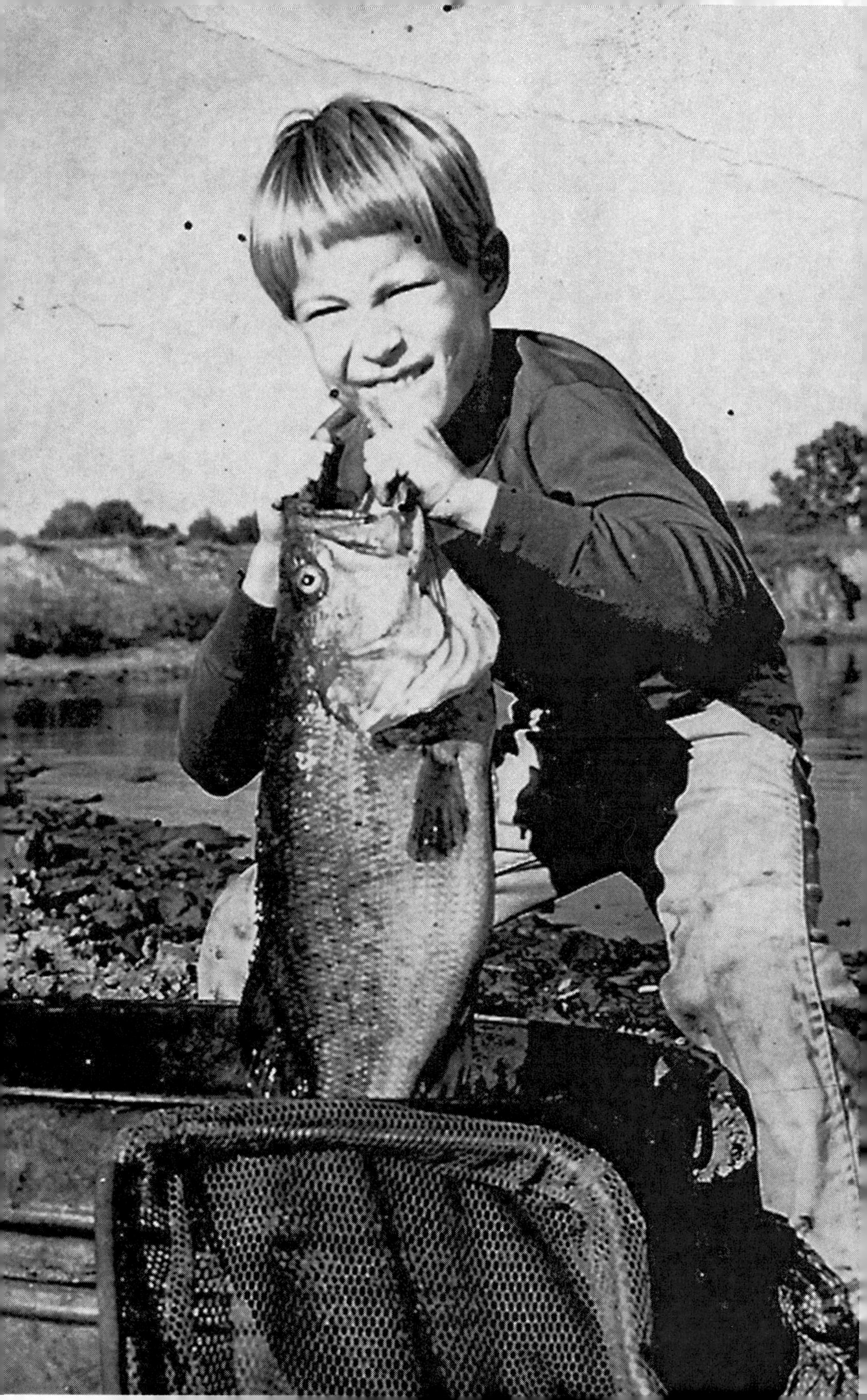

Pick-up man

Most southern outdoorsmen start out as pick-up men. This term does not relate to one's lack of marital status nor to vehicular choices. It is a term that applies to the lowest level of the hunting fraternity and is the first step, the beginning, so to speak, of a hunter's career. It is an honor to be asked to perform this duty, and a prerequisite for one who aspires to carry his or her own gun. The tour of duty starts at the opening of dove season, and lasts for one full year, at which time a pick-up man is considered knowledgeable enough to carry a gun, with hawk-like supervision, in the presence of others.

My own duty began on September 1, 1966. It was Unkoo's first dove hunt of the year, and the anticipation had been building for weeks. First we had to get the corn cut into silage and stored in the silos. The harvest was somewhat delayed by my Uncle Hugh's insistence that "blinds" of standing corn be left at strategic locations all around the field. Next, wheat was "planted" or "top-sowed" over a third of the field every week, for three weeks. The next part, my favorite, was a daily check on the bird population which involved hurtling down the cut corn rows in a pickup truck, with the horn blaring.

As September approached, the birds flocked to our field in droves and the daily census revealed grey clouds of darting and twisting doves that would rise and circle, only to re-alight, after we had passed.

The long awaited day finally came and a select group of intrepid sportsmen and women congregated at the entrance to the field. Noon is the start time for Tennessee's opening and it is usually a few hours later before the birds begin to move, so there is no hurry to get out in the hot sun. Most people chose to stay in the shade of the giant oaks, near the road, and "catch up" for, what was for many, the first time since last year. A few nimrods sallied forth, in the hopes of securing a prime location, while the less anxious, or more experienced, would casually sip on a cool drink, discuss the current events of the day, and keep a wary eye on the skies.

I was of the first group, but assigned to the latter, that year. I wanted to go where the shooting was but my "Gun" was content to wait for the flight in the shade. Every half hour Unkoo would drive around the field and offer cold drinks, water or Cokes, to the guests. These Cokes were the small, six- ounce bottles with the fixed cap; the ones that tasted better than any since, and my job was to ride in the back of the truck, open them with a bottle opener, and pass them out. It was incredibly hot and those Cokes, as they came out of a cooler full of crushed ice that had been sloshing around in the back of the truck, gave meaning to the term- "ice cold."

Eventually, about three o'clock, Unkoo said, "Well monster, lets go see what we can do." I was quivering like a young lab, first cold front in November.

Unkoo took a stand where a tree line led up to the field from the Nonconna Creek bottoms and there was plenty of open ground in front of us for the birds to fall in. "Doves like to follow a fence or tree line when moving from resting to feeding areas," he said, " and if there is a dead tree around they will go to it first, to check out the field before dropping in to feed." This spot had both and we settled down to await our first customers.

Unkoo shot a 12 gauge Fox side by side. It was an ejector model and had two sets of barrels. The short barrels, twenty-six inches long with improved cylinder on the right and slightly tighter on the left, were for quail. The long barrels were thirty-inch with modified on the right and full on the left and the gun had double triggers so that he could easily choose a barrel. For doves, he shot the long barrels with one ounce of 7 ½ shot. Back then, the shells had paper hulls and traveled at about 1100 fps. The smell of those spent paper hulls is one of the most exquisite, memory provoking smells, in all of a sporting lifetime. To this day, whenever I find myself in the proximity of a newly fired paper hull, I pick it up and smell it. Immediately I am transported back to a younger, more wondrous time and place, where everything is new and emotion runs deep.

Once settled on his folding stool, he instructed me to squat beside him and about a half step back to be out of his peripheral vision. I was admonished not to get in front of the gun while he was shooting and not to go until he sent me. I was a bit over-eager and had to be cautioned not to move while doves were approaching. "You don't have to hide from doves. But they can see motion, any motion, so you have to be still."

The first bird came from the field and he dropped it cleanly, with one shot, out in the open. As I marveled at what I had just seen the command came, "Go git 'im Monster!" and I took off. The bird fluttered its death throws out in the corn stalks enabling me to locate it easily. It was the most beautiful blue-grey color I had ever seen and I marveled at its smooth perfection. Sleek, powerful, intricate and frail, were all packaged into this one form. When I picked it up I could almost feel God's hand at work in the making of this wondrous creature. A drop of blood from it's beak reminded me that we had killed it, and I felt remorse for this, but excitement too. I carried it back by the long tail and set it gently down in the grass. Birds were flying steadily now and guns were popping in all directions, but Unkoo was not shooting, he was watching me.

"Lets try and get some more," he said. Remorse quickly cast aside, I jumped into my position as if it were a track meet. The next couple of birds were singles, as before, and I concentrated on speed. Eventually, I learned to mark the birds down, with some instruction, and to "Never take your eye off of them if you can help it." On doubles, I learned to pick out an odd shaped stalk, or weed, in the vicinity of each bird, and not to move until I had done so. The doves blended in perfectly with the weeds and corn stubble and practice was the only way to get good at finding them.

All too soon we had "the limit," which was ten at the time, and I felt a giant swell of pride that "we" had done it. "Carry the gun back to the truck, Monster, I'll get the birds." Wow, I get to hold the gun? Unkoo proceeded to show me how to open it, and carry it that way. He explained that the only truly safe way to carry a gun was open, and unloaded, and everyone could see that it was safe. As he reached for his stool he said, "Lets go see how our guests are doing." I headed for the truck with the open gun held in front of me and felt like I was Stanley, in Africa.

Our round in the pickup showed us that many of the better shots were done, and most were plucking their birds. In those days doves were plucked, not breasted, a tradition that I still participate in from time to time.

As we came back to the parking area, Unkoo told me that he wanted me to retrieve for my grandfather, who was just setting up under a tree up ahead. "Remember what you have learned," I was told, "and pay attention."

Well, I loved my grandfather but I thought he was too old to hunt. I told Unkoo that I wanted to retrieve for somebody who could shoot. He chuckled a little and told me to just go on down there "you might be surprised."

I hiked down to his tree and told Granddaddy what I was there for. He said that was an excellent idea because he couldn't bend over too well, "This steel hip I got in the war, it slows me down."

It didn't slow his shooting any, as far as I could tell. In the next few minutes I was witness to an exhibition of skill the likes of which I was never to experience again. He knocked his birds down two at a time, and refrained from shooting at singles. The little Model 21, 20 gauge, with the long barrels, would bark twice, so close together it almost sounded like one shot, and two puffs of feathers would be left, hanging in the still, hot air. Unlike Unkoo, Granddaddy shot standing up. He explained that one should shoot sitting or standing, but don't try to stand and then shoot. "It throws off your timing," he said, "Besides, it takes me too long to stand up." Wide eyed, I nodded and kept quiet.

When we were through, which didn't take very long, Granddaddy asked if I would like to shoot his gun. Boy-howdy I sure did! He had me place a can on the ground about twenty paces away, and showed me how to load the gun. "Never point the gun at yourself or anyone else," he said. "Even if it is unloaded, you treat it like it is loaded, all the time."

"Yes sir," I replied.

"When you shoot a shotgun, you always keep both eyes open. You aim a rifle, you point a shotgun." I lined up the side-by-side and squeezed her off, as instructed. The resulting blast nearly knocked me over but the can exploded into a gnarled mass blown several yards down the turn-row. "Go pick it up and look at it," he said, "be careful not to cut yourself." The destructive power of the close range blast was awesome. "Take a good look at it," he said, "that is what would happen to a friend or family member if you were ever careless with a shotgun." It was a lesson I hope I never forget.

Throughout that fall I was pick-up-man for just about everyone in the family, at one time or another. They all added to my instruction, and most of the time I got to shoot their gun at something, one time, after they were through.

That Christmas, under the tree, was the best present I will ever get- my own gun. It was the most beautiful gun that was ever made, a single barrel, side-lever 410, totally devoid of engraving or artwork, and it was mine. The stock had been cut down to accommodate my stature, and it had a case. I think that during the first few days under my ownership, it probably spent less than an hour in the case, and I probably cleaned it a dozen times.

For the next year, no trip to the country was complete without a box of shells and some clay targets. Unkoo had a spring thrower, mounted on a heavy wooden pallet, and spent countless hours cocking the heavy spring and launching targets over the rail fence behind the cabin. At first, after a session, I would hop through the fence and pick up the unbroken targets to use again. There were many. The twenty-six inch full choked barrel only allowed for a solid hit, or a full miss. But as the summer progressed, there were less and less unbroken ones. He had me stand at different angles, and each time it was like starting over, but eventually, I would get the hang of it.

At long last it was time to try the real thing. Our field that year was big. Way out in the middle, and out of gunshot range of anyone else, there was an old, dead snag. Around it had been left a few stalks of standing corn and a few tall weeds. On opening day, at one o'clock, I was dropped off at this spot with eight boxes of shells and admonished not to shoot low and not to shoot myself. Shooting low, a real no-no in a dove field with other hunters present was strictly forbidden. Failure to abide this rule was the surest way not to get invited back to anybody's dove shoot. I wasn't going to break it. It was odd, though, that my spot was so far away from everyone else.

The doves came at me in droves that day, and I think that area must have been "salted," for those of you who might know what that means. I fired at everything that came by. My gun became blistering hot and burned my hands but still I continued to blast away- and nothing fell. I had shot seven boxes of shells, the ground was covered with spent hulls and I was bruised and flinching badly when Unkoo drove up in the pickup. I was about to cry as I stood there while he took in the situation.

"Jump in the truck, Monster, bring your gun, you need a break and there's someone I want you to meet."

Man, I could feel that ice-cold Coca-Cola all the way to my toes as we rode across the field and back towards the old silo, where everyone had gathered.

I soon realized that they were all through. I was the last one still in the field. No one asked me how I had done, it was written on my face.

Unkoo was talking to someone I didn't know and gestured for me to come over there. "This is your cousin, Mr. Nash Buckingham. He is a very famous shot and is going to teach you how to hit one." I was a little scared of this big, tall man, with his kaki shirt and tie, and the big black patch over one eye. When he spoke, he immediately dispelled my fears with his kind and knowing manner. "Have you got a gun Buck?"

"Yes sir!"

"You know, my name is Buck too. Go get your gun and we'll go shoot a dove." I went back to the truck and asked Unkoo if I could take my gun out with Mr. Buck. He said that was fine and to be safe and remember what I had been taught.

I broke the 410 open and carefully walked back through the crowd to where Mr. Buck waited on the other side of the silo. He was watching the field when I arrived, and, after a minute or two, he looked my way and said; "Now Buck, the first thing you need to do is watch the birds. Doves fly in patterns in any field. I've been standing here for a while. Every now and then a bird flies that far fence line and cuts across that low place in the field." I followed his arm as he explained the route. "Then they come right by this silo and out the gap in the trees." I nodded, beginning to get the picture. "The easiest shot is one coming right over you, so we are going to stand right in front of that gap, and shoot a bird." I was willing, but nervous. Mr. Buck sounded so confident that it was hard not to believe him. "Now, first off, I don't want you to load your gun" he said. "See that dove flying down the fence?"

"Yes sir."

"Put your gun up and follow him; here he comes across; keep following… coming right at you… your going to shoot him …right…THERE!" I did as I was told, and I could see every detail on that bird. I might could have got him! Mr. Buck continued the instruction, "All you have to do is keep the gun right on him, and when I say, 'NOW!' cover him up and pull the trigger. Now Let's load up and try it." I put one of the long, three-inch, paper hulls in and closed the gun. Mr. Buck and I only stood there for a few minutes before he saw one coming on the right path. "This will be our customer, so cock your gun and get on him, but don't pull the trigger till I tell you." I followed the bird as it came closer and closer; when it was almost over me, but still a little in front, he said, "NOW!," and I pulled the trigger. The bird came down at a fluttering slant and I almost beat it to the ground. Mr. Buck was laughing as he picked my gun up out of the dust. At least I remembered to open it before I threw it down. "Nice shot Buck, I believe you've got the hang of it!" And so I had.

Thus, like so many before me, I graduated from the rank of pick-up man and into the annals of history as a full fledged hunter, and, like most of you who have made the transition in the time honored traditional fashion, I wouldn't have it any other way.

The cutting of silage was always a big to do and came at just the right time for dove season!

Hugh E. Buckingham, gentleman, sportsman, and a crack shot.

Training Days

Like sands through the hourglass, so pass the days of our lives. If one were to look closely at the bottom of the glass, with a magnifier of some sort, you would see that no two grains are the same. Occasionally, one would be brighter than any around it. For an avid outdoorsman, looking back to the early years, these would be "training days," the days that held important memories that helped shape one's life. Often you would not have known of their significance at the time but memory recall keeps flashing them back into our heads as a reminder.

It was 1968 or thereabout and first frosts had seared the rolling hills and tinted the mighty oaks. Bobwhite's polt rearing duties were over and the strong, young birds were formed into new coveys, with established territories, that whistled their gathering at dusk. Time was upon us, Unkoo and I, to get the bird dogs in shape. This was before the age of four-wheelers, GPS collars, and electronic beepers. We carried whistles, and we walked.

It took a lot of concentration, and sometimes, some hustle. You had to know where the dogs were at all times. If one disappeared into a deep, briar-choked gulley, chances were, it was on point. A good pointer has to know that if it does its job, you will find it— no matter what. Dogs that get lost learn to flush their birds after a time.

You learn a lot about dogs if you really focus on them as they go about their jobs. Concurrently, you learn a lot about people at the same time. Breeding shows in all of God's creatures, and I would have to include Man in that group. A good bird dog is driven to find birds. It will run itself nearly to death doing it, and ignore cuts, scratches, burs, thorns and the weather. His only request is that you come find him, and flush the birds, so he can go searching for more. This same phenomena will lead a man to walk for hours, past being tired and sore, to get a shot at a bevy, or get him up way before daylight, day after day, in order to be where the ducks are by first shooting light.

We are all subject to our genetic code and some of us are hunters, plain and simple.

That year, as dog training days turned into shooting days, and skill level with firearm progressed, albeit slowly, Unkoo asked if I would like to go duck hunting! I was so excited that sleep became difficult for quite some time.

A pair of hip boots, supposedly insulated, with rubber straps to go around one's belt, and a green plastic "Duck Commander" duck call with lanyard, were advanced pre-Christmas and birthday. Hours were spent "talking" to the tame ducks on Chickasaw Lake or practicing at the end of our driveway, after Mom banished the duck call from the house. No waking moment found me without the duck call on my person, school and church included. Unkoo always said that "No boy should ever be caught without a pocket knife and some fishing line," to this list I added the duck call.

Unkoo's duck club was located near Wynne, Arkansas, and was a classic green-timber set up called "Murray's Woods." During October of every year water was pumped into the woods via deep wells in the surrounding rice fields. Predominantly oak timber, acorns abounded, but contrary to popular opinion, ducks don't eat acorns all that often. They do eat rice—A LOT! Nighttime feeding mallards with craws stuffed full of rice would swarm the tree tops, right at daylight, looking for the rest and seclusion of the timber.

That first morning can only be described as one of wonder and awe. Mom made me put on my flannel pajamas over the Sears Roebuck, white cotton long johns, and then four pairs of cotton socks to fill up my boots. She topped the outfit off with a pair of those brown, cotton, gardeners gloves, that have been around since Hominids first crossed the Bering Straight. I was stuffed so tight that my arms stood straight out and my toes curled up in the fashion of the Japanese Geisha Girls. She said I would need it all, and I believed her.

If I close my eyes I can still smell the little shack where we had our pre-dawn gathering before the hunt. The odor of coffee, wood smoke, canvas, and old rubber mixed with the earthy smells of gumbo mud and damp vegetation. I think there were five men in the group that morning, besides us, and I can remember at least two of their names; Bobby Haverty, because he was an excellent shot and good duck caller, and "Hubert," who did duty as guide/caller for the group. He blew a green, "Duck Commander," and to this day, is the best "woods caller" I have ever heard.

Boots, coats, and gloves were donned before stepping out into the biting chill of pre-dawn darkness.

Stars studded the night sky above the rusty tin roof and invisible wing beats could be heard, along with faint whistles, and chatter. A short walk down the muddy road brought us to the edge of the water, and deep, dark, cathedral-like timber. The men, all wearing chest waders, struck off down the trail at what seemed to me, an exceedingly fast pace. Within a few minutes, on tiptoes because the water was perilously close to the top of my boots, I stepped in a stump hole and down I went. Piercing, stinging, cold, attacked, like I had never experienced before, as layer upon layer of clothing succumbed to infiltration. Unkoo held my gun as I held a tree and tried to alternately lift my legs up high enough to empty the heavy boots of water. It should be noted here, that this is an inferior method that is no longer recommended. The water tends to run up under your clothing and contact other body parts that were previously dry. He then asked me if I wanted to go back–and got a resounding "Nooo!" for an answer. Off we went again, with a caution to "take your time and keep moving, you'll warm up," and sure enough, the soaked-up water began to warm, and become tolerable.

When we reached the "hole" it was before legal shooting time and I was given instructions to "get behind a tree, keep your head down, and don't move until I tell you." The ducks were starting to fill the sky above us and the men opened up with their calls and began kicking and splashing the water to simulate live duck activity. Soon the hole began to fill up with waterfowl. Hundreds at a time tried to squeeze through the opening in the trees and were silhouetted against a faintly lighter sky. The beating of their wings made the air pulse around me and hundreds of ducks, mostly mallards, swam around my shivering form, preening and calling just feet away.

Shooting time arrived, the sitting ducks were flushed, and the order to "load up!" was given. I asked my uncle if I should call. He said, "Not while any ducks are around. Too many calls, like too many cooks, spoils the broth." I knew that was just a nice way to say no, but I was dying to give it a try on wild ducks.

Soon a vast tornado of mallards swirled round and round our hole in the woods and as the leaders filtered down through the trees, more piled in behind them. When suspense was almost too great to bear, the order came– "Take Em!" I swang into the mass and "POP," the 410 went off, answered by the crash of the men's big 12's. When it was over, Unkoo asked if I had killed anything.

Somewhat embarrassed, all I could say was, "I'm not sure."

It seems that there was, or is, an unwritten rule that kids always get to shoot first in these situations, and always are made to feel successful. These gentlemen sportsmen quickly convinced me that several of the largest, fattest, greenheads bore 7½ pellets from my gun. One went so far as to explain to me that "This one threw his head back when you shot. When they get hit with a 12 gauge, they always throw their head forward." Made sense to me, maybe I did get one!

All too soon, the two duck limit was nearly acquired, mostly greenheads, and it was decided that I was to call and shoot solo on the last duck. The men moved back into the timber a little and started telling stories and what-not while I moved up to the edge of the hole. I was calling, and kicking the water as I had seen them do, but I wasn't seeing much. It's hard to see much while not moving and keeping your head down behind a tree. I didn't realize that instructions could change with different circumstances. Suddenly I heard a rushing noise, glanced up, and saw a green-winged teal barreling straight out of the stratosphere. It looked like he might hit me if I didn't do something—fast. With the reflexes that only the very young possess, I cocked my gun, shoved the barrel at the teal, and pulled the trigger. My first solo duck exploded into an inedible mass, and I was hooked for life.

When we got back to the cabin, the men sat by the pot-bellied stove and drank coffee. After squeezing some of the water out of my clothes, I slipped out and snuck a little piece down the road to the "rest pond." This area of the club was so named because it was never shot over and provided a safe haven for wintering waterfowl. I crawled up the levee, and wriggled into a briar thicket unobserved by the ducks that were already there and began to call softly to them, and watch their reactions. My training days were not over.

Flash forward a bit, to the end of the season. Unkoo and I were making the long drive homeward from Wynne. I had been noticing a good many things, not the least of which was that I wanted more gun. Glancing a little bit his way I sheepishly asked, "Unkoo, can I get a gun that shoots more than one time?" He grinned a little at that one, kind of like he knew it was coming.

"When you can kill a limit of doves with that gun, I'll get you another." Well now, talk about throwing down the gauntlet!

Jump forward again to September, the following year. It is the opening day of dove season and I am knee-deep in spent 410 hulls. Nine beautiful, sleek, grey doves are meticulously lined up on the ground beside me and I only have one to go. I see Unkoo's truck coming into my part of the field and I know it is time to quit. Frantic, I scan the skies one last time and zero in on a lone, red-winged black bird, flittering along at the limit of my range. Hammer cocked, a long forward allowance, and bang, down he came. I hurried to retrieve because the truck was almost there and when Unkoo arrived I proudly proclaimed, "I got my limit!"

He chuckled a bit as I loaded my "limit" in the back of the truck, and again as I showed my mom and dad a nice, clean, picked limit, of ten birds. That night, at home, we had my "doves" for dinner and I'm pretty sure Mom ate the black bird and never said a word.

True to his word, the following Christmas morn found a side-by-side Ithaca 20 gauge, twenty-eight inch barrels choked improved and modified, with three-inch chambers, under the tree. That very afternoon I shot my first two quail (I had never been able to get one with the full choked 410), and the next morning a limit of mallards that I was dead certain that I had shot myself. I felt as if I had the power of an atomic bomb in my hands, and the indelible lesson seared into my brain was this- "A good big gun out shoots a good little gun, every time."

The education and training of a sportsman never stops, and it is not always about guns and dogs. Important aspects of wildlife management, care of equipment, manners and customs, are learned during outings and in between. Fishing has its' own set of rules and customs. One usually starts out with cane poles, then casting rods, and for those with an artistic bent, a fly rod. But, there is a whole nother fishing world out there for the adventuresome, namely big game. And so the day finally came when my uncle, the consummate mentor, decided to let me into this world with some very different training days, in Yucatan.

The first thing I realized upon landing at the small airport in Meridith, was that I had not paid nearly enough attention in Spanish class. Uncle Hugh had a little book put out by the border patrol that he consulted constantly, but I didn't think "Halto!" or "Arriba los Manos!" was all that helpful.

A small, rusty looking airplane brought us the final leg into Isla Aguada del Carmen, and on the approach I noticed a lot of crashed planes and blown up military equipment. Unkoo explained that these were remnants of past battles having to do with the disputed outcomes of soccer matches between each town or region. I made a mental note not to mention soccer while I was here.

The Island had a village on it, the inhabitants of which seemed to scratch out a living catching huge sharks in nets, out of small, tippy looking boats, sometimes with unreliable sounding propulsion. It is interesting to note that we were told that most inhabitants did not even know how to swim, a testament to the shark population in that area. On the other end of the island was a camp for "sportsmen" called, "El Tarpon Tropical." A self-styled "New York Jew," named Andy, had left the hustles and bustles of the big apple and moved to the bush. He ran a clean, thatched roof camp, with courteous guides, good food and uncrowded fishing waters... and tarpon, lots of tarpon.

The first morning found us both on the beach doing what was to become a daily routine– catching "jacks." At daylight, large schools of jack crevalle, in the two to four pound class, drive baitfish on to the beach and can be caught via casting rod and jig. The purpose of this exercise was to secure bait, in order to catch the hardhead catfish which were, in turn, used to catch the tarpon. I marveled at the bulldog strength and ferocity of these jacks, and couldn't imagine anything that could fight harder.

When enough jacks were secured, and buried in the sand where the sea gulls couldn't strip them of usable flesh, we went in to a breakfast of fresh mangoes, papaya, eggs, and some sort of fish.

The guides arrived about then and ran their heavy wooden boats onto the beach. These men were small, wiry looking fellows with straw hats and semi-white cotton clothing, barefoot, and definitely "no habla Engless." Their boats carried two outboard motors apiece. No boat that I saw had two that matched in either horsepower or markings, and they were all tiller-handle. These dexterous fellows just stood by the transom and drove with their knees and both hands.

Emanuel was our guide and let us know that we needed the big outfits for "grande sabalo," which meant big tarpon. I was sent running up from the beach for a couple of stiff outfits, with Penn reels, and lots of thirty pound line.

Next, he motored our clunky craft up the beach a little ways, while at the same time cutting up jack crevallia into one inch cubes. At a somehow predetermined spot in the ocean, he cut the engines and we caught catfish, us with rod and reel, and he with a hand line wrapped around a stick and two hooks. Emanuel could cast as far as I could with a sixteen inch stick. The catfish stored in a plain bucket, (no aerator), and we were off to "the passes."

Unkoo did the rigging while we were in transit, and I tried to assist. An egg sinker, three ounces or more, was threaded on the main line, followed by a five foot Bimini twist with a swivel at the end, and then four feet of one hundred pound test leader with a large, stout J-hook. Upon arrival at the fishing grounds, an eight to ten inch catfish is carefully grabbed out of the bucket, de-spined with pliers, and impaled through the lips. Everyone who has ever dealt with hardhead catfish has been stabbed, and my hands were swollen for days. Once we had the catfish frisking on the bottom the work was done, and we could begin reeling in tarpon, or so I thought.

Big, silver backed fish were rolling all around the boat in the turbid water, but it was several minutes before we saw any action. Unkoo's bait was taken first and he handed it to me. The clicker on the reel was going strong, and I was instructed to count to ten, engage the reel, and set the hook three times as hard as I could. On the very first "set" the world went into overdrive and I thought I was tied to a cruise missile. "Old bucket mouth" screamed off a hundred yards of line, tail-walked twice, and cleared the water by a good six feet or more, all in the first five seconds. It was twenty minutes before I gained any appreciable line back and a solid hour before Emanuel sunk a gaff through Sabalo's lower jaw.

Wow, that was a fight to remember. We fished for seven days like that, and caught dozens of tarpon, some over a hundred pounds. We caught grouper, permit, sharks, and barracuda, usually after catching a couple of tarpon. You see, tarpon fight so hard that you really don't want to catch more than one or two a day. Your arms and hands cramp up and it is time to do something easier, like casting or trolling for smaller fish.

Acres of sand and quite a few big fish have passed through the hourglass since that day, but that was my introduction to big game in the salt. We killed that first fish, and the photo I still have shows a bucktoothed pre-teen of sixty-eight pounds, standing in the sand next to a seventy-two pound silver king. That was a training day to remember.

Moments pass and so do the years. Bright memories stand out: Cold, sunny days with sparkling ice rings around the trees–great shots!—infamous misses!—a hilltop point with a picture perfect back—a young pups' first find—steamy heat and more battles with leviathans of the salt—kind words of instruction and camaraderie that can only be found within the blood sports.

There came a day when I wandered afield alone. Despair clutched at my insides with desperate strength. My mind wouldn't stay away from the gloom and I had to get OUT, walk, focus on the dogs, in order to stay sane. You see, my uncle had died. Closest companion of fourteen years and mentor in all the things I loved most...gone...forever.

Mom and dad were sympathetic to my request not to attend the funeral. They dropped me off at the farm that afternoon with Suzy and Queenie- my dogs now. I had some thinking to do. First, I circled around through birdless country to get the wind right for the better area...how did I know to do that? Suzy locked up on the wood-lot covey in sparse cover. They were going to flush wild so I was careful going in. On the rise, I killed a bird with the right barrel and let the rest go—too early in the season to pound a covey... how did I know that, I wondered? The dreary grey skies that I had not even noticed that day suddenly parted. A blue-sky patch appeared overhead and beautiful rays of sunshine bathed the wood lot and surrounding pastureland. Realization came like a stroke of lightning... He was here; he was with me, and the dogs. He was in the air all around me and even in my mind. All that he had taught me, and all the love and attention he bestowed upon me were mine forever. I could miss him, I could cry a little, or just be sad sometimes, but his love of the outdoors had transferred to me. I knew at that moment that everything was going to be OK and I could actually feel his approval of the decision.

Hugh L. Buckingham died in the fall of 1974, from a rare and painful form of nerve cancer that had been with him for most of his life. He was forty-nine years old. I can say without fear of contradiction that he gave of the things that matter in life more than he received. Gone but not forgotten! God bless him.

"We killed the first one"

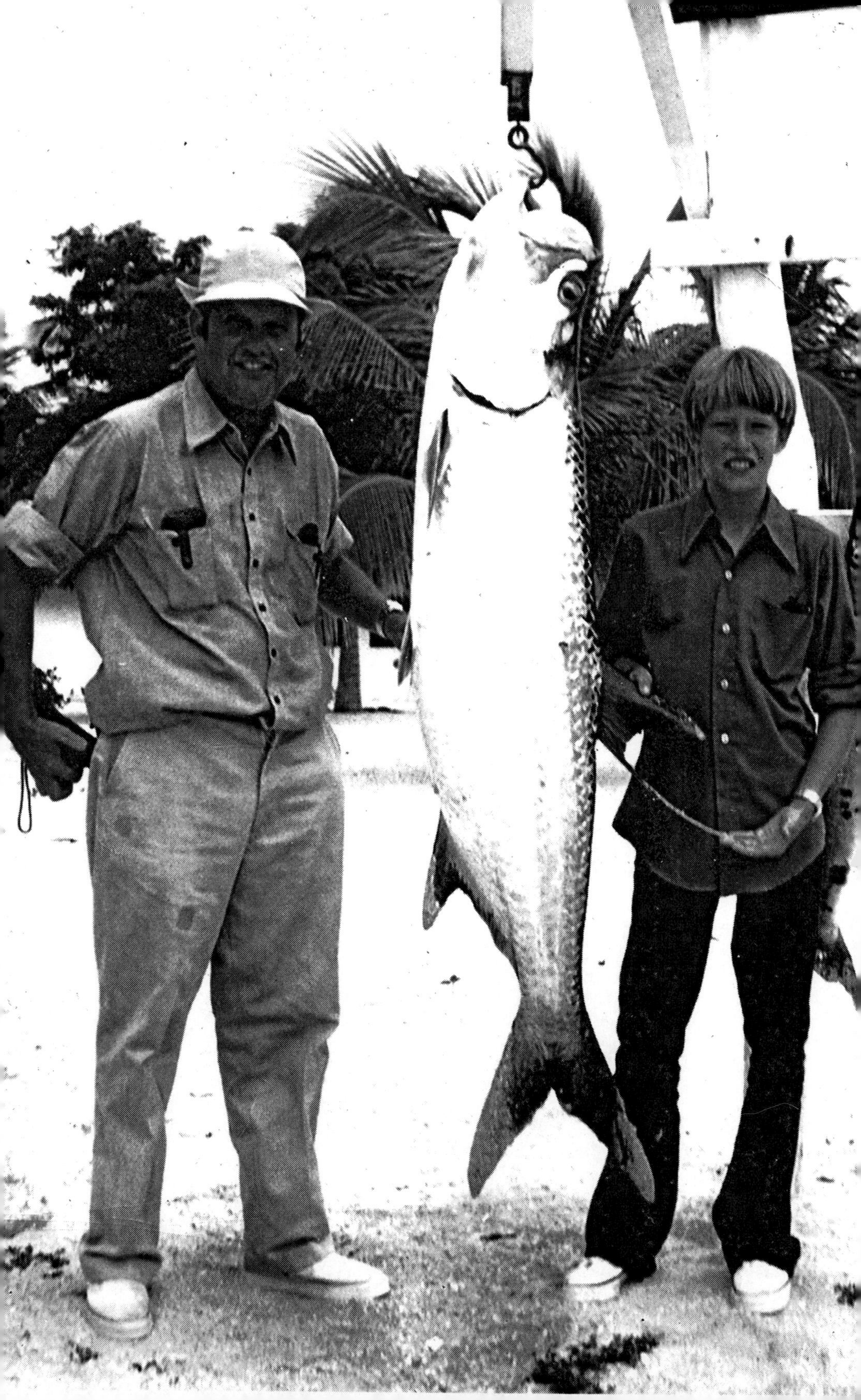

Mistletoe

The two boys, aged about twelve and feeling very "grown-up" and ready for independence, left the battered old white suburban at a point where the steep sided bayou came close to the dirt road. They had their backpacks, the same ones used for school, Crossman .177 caliber pellet rifles, belt knives, canteens, and of course snacks. They were also loaded down with BB's. The .177 caliber air guns would shoot the much less expensive BB's just fine and history had proven, time and again, that their average daily expenditure of ammunition was grossly embarrassing.

The proposed "expedition," thought up by a benevolent parent who probably secretly suppressed a desire for carefree adolescence himself, was to scout out new country for turkey season, and report back. The bayou ran a circuitous route through some of the deepest, darkest woods on North Lake Hunting Club and they were to walk the length of it, living off the land, and get picked up at the other end at dark. The two took the job seriously, but with some trepidation. You see, this was Mississippi River bottomland, about as wild as it gets in the South, and they were totally on their own, in strange country.

As parental control receded into the distance, they were admonished to "follow the bayou, and if you lose it, use your compass to head east until you strike it again." They pushed onward, heads held high and weapons carried at port-arms position, into the unknown.

Neither of the two knew what turkey sign looked like, but they scanned the forest floor anyway, with grim determination.

They did recognize a cotton mouth, and forty-five minutes of solid pounding, first with BB's and then clubs, reduced the serpent into a much more benevolent state. They took what was left of the head and milked the poison out like they had seen done on "Mutual of Omaha's Wild Kingdom." Next it was decided to save the skin as a trophy. The beginning stages of the taxidermial process revealed several hundred holes in the skin, rendering it unusable. Live and learn.

Back on the march and down into the watercourse, where tracks were more prevalent. Possum, coon, deer, turtle, fox and beaver- it was all there to be deciphered. Much crawling and sneaking—BB's glancing off of sunning turtle shells—a prize! An eastern three-toed box turtle with vibrant yellow dots—carried for a while and then released. Careful sneaks were made on what they called, "gawks," which were actually the ever vigilant great blue herons—inevitable failure with the great birds taking to wing and alarming everything

MISTLETOE

in the woods with their loud croaking, GAWK-GAWK-GAWWWK. Next, a hornet's nest! Careful aiming and much expenditure of ammunition—it falls—RUN!—RUN! ... Look, mistletoe! BB's wasted, a tree to be climbed, much hacking, down it comes—our parents can use this for Christmas decoration!—into the packs it goes.

It was getting late in the afternoon and they didn't know how far they had to go. The general turning over of logs and trying to dig up armadillos ceased, and travel became more determined. When they came out on the road it was still daylight but the suburban was already there. The benevolent parent questioned the two boys closely and listened with real interest as the events of the day came pouring out in rapid, high-pitched voices. When they were done, and had showed off their spoils, mainly a few old turtle shells, some bones, and the mistletoe, an idea began to form, which caused a grin to appear on the man's face. He had an idea that would further the boys' education in a different way... a capitalistic way.

He told the boys that he had been driving around for several hours, and that he had seen a ton of mistletoe in the trees. Christmas was only a couple of months away and he thought the boys could sell all that they could get there hands on. A meeting was held right there on the spot, the partnership was incorporated, deadlines set for the second weekend in December, product identified, and marketing plan secured.

Fall rolled on, in its' usual fashion, with the normal demands and activities, but the two young capitalists did not forget the plan to raise some "real cash money."

On the appointed day, with all in readiness, they set out for the bottoms.

After the first few attempts at climbing, and cutting the whole limb down with a saw, the shotgun method was employed. The two boys would stand back and blast a clump of mistletoe, with their single barrel shotguns, and pick up the bigger pieces that fell down. This had a tendency to knock all the berries off but was infinitely more exciting and, of course, time-efficient.

When the back of the suburban was literally crammed with loose sprigs and whole bunches, it was time to go into packaging mode. Single sprigs went in a ziploc and were priced at a whole dollar. Multiple sprigs in a ziploc went for five dollars, and a whole clump for twenty.

Marketing and delivery were simultaneous, a streamlined process. A red wagon was procured, hair was combed and festive sweaters donned, and the two boys went door to door, perfecting their salesmanship along the way. In no time flat they sold out, netting several hundred dollars. This was a veritable fortune at the time and the two were ecstatic.

Over the following years and decades the two capitalists tried many methods of cash accrual. The usual lawn mowing, painting, and fencing occurred. Lifeguarding, firewood cutting and even a short venture into the Gulf Coast shrimping business were attempted (a difficult proposition when one lives 500 miles from the gulf). I think it fair to say, that neither one of them ever had a better job, than mistletoe.

Hatchie Coon Rules

My dad was a kind and loving person. He had inner strength of character combined with a keen intelligence, capable and willing to tackle any new problem. As an Ivy League graduate, physician, and cancer research pioneer, he was at the top of the class. He was not a hunter. Most of the time, the general direction of people's lives is set at an early age. Chance, opportunity, and availability play a big part.

Daddy, as if he didn't have enough demands on his time, decided to join a duck club, for me. His old-time friend, Chuck Berry, recommended a club up in northeast Arkansas, about an hour and a half by car from Memphis. Mr. Berry was a member there and could "show us the ropes." The club had an Indian name, Hatchie Coon, which meant "dark water."

My first glimpse of the club came in about 1974. We followed directions north from Memphis, through the rice lands of Arkansas, past Wapanocca, took a right at Tulot, and then the long gravel road eventually ending at the levee beyond which lie the fabled "Sunken Lands" of the St. Francis River. Giant oaks, hickory, and cypress of a girth and height unobtainable in other locals, stretched beyond visible ken. The sight did then, and always shall, send a jolt of adrenaline through my system– sharpening senses– tingling extremities. It is a deep down recognition inherited with the DNA from another age and time.

Within this same view of vast forest fastness, stretched a single narrow line of clearing, so long that it vanished into nothingness. Centered within this clearing, as if born of infinity, ran a set of gleaming railroad tracks. Far out, almost indiscernible in the shadows, was a VW bus fitted with railroad wheels, and noisily approaching.

Mr. Hoots, who operated this contraption, was the club manager. A shade over six feet, white haired, probably in his late sixties, he had a gigantic upward-curled walrus mustache, a twinkling eye, and infallible good humor. He regaled us with "earthy" stories of GI life in Europe during his service in WWII on the long, slow, clacking, trek to the clubhouse. I'm sure my dad wished for some earplugs for me, while I, on the other hand, tried not to miss a word.

The clubhouse, the third I believe on that site, and all lost to the ravages of unchecked fire, was a configuration of trailers built up on a mound about twelve feet above ground level. This was not an undo precaution as we soon found out that the mighty St. Francis could, and would, inundate this whole country with great regularity, and, at times, great depth. There was a guide house built on stilts nearby, a pump house for fuel, numerous boats of all ages and designs, many of which were hand-made wooden masterpieces, reminiscent of a bygone era. Further out in the woods were a live-pigeon ring and a skeet range, both carved out of, and enveloped by, massive, tall timber. The clubhouse mound sat about 200 yards from the river and a canal ran from the river to a boat landing at its base. A very tall, rickety, pier went from the back door of the clubhouse, down the south side of the canal, and ended at a floating dock on the river. About halfway down, and also elevated, was an area for members' lockers, a duck picking room, and general storage.

My dad and I fell in love with the place. Mrs. Hoots was a fabulous cook, and she prided herself on making sure that fourteen year-old boys had enough to eat. The fishing was excellent, both in the river for catfish and Kentucky bass, and in the "project" for crappie, goggle-eye, and large-mouths. The dove shoots were legendary, squirrels, bullfrogs, and furbearers abounded, and opportunities for duck hunting were limitless. I say limitless, because this place was huge! Although the club only owned a few hundred acres, it was situated right smack in the middle of the St. Francis Sunken Lands. Miles and miles in any direction were open to public hunting with the river and all it's channels, runs, and bayous winding throughout. For a young boy with any inclination to explore, this place was heaven... with a gun.

Our joining of the club only gave us a few weekends to explore before the opening day of duck season. The club maintained about a dozen duck blinds on the river, and with the aid of a large wall map in the clubhouse, I had been able to locate most of these, but as the big day approached, we didn't have a clue where to go or how to hunt in this new situation.

Dad hired a guide. We met the fellow on opening-eve and he seemed nice. Tall and lean, sun-browned and quiet, he said that he hoped we killed a "whole boat-load of ducks tomorrow." Now wait a minute, the limit was four (if I remember correctly), and that would be bad. This guy was an outlaw! What had we gotten ourselves into? I couldn't sleep, and worried all night that we might not be able to stop this guy from being a game hog.

Well, as it turned out, I was not to be bothered by any morality issues or problems of conscience. Dad had drawn "Dr. Cocke's" blind, which was located just about a mile upriver on the inside bend, just before you get to O. J. James' famous blind, "The Suck Hole." We had about seventy-five decoys out, arranged with a big opening running lengthwise through the middle of the spread. This opening, which one would normally think was for the ducks to work into, was actually to let all the boat traffic through our decoys without damage. There were a few panicky looking ducks flying around, and we called to them, but they were mostly intent on not getting too close to the water and getting run over. During the occasional lull in traffic, the aptly named

"Suck Hole" would thunder out a tremendous volley, followed by numerous cripple shots and the sounds of retrieving by boat. As far as I could tell, they didn't even call.

Our guide, whose name I believe was Ray, or something like that, said that he had another place, and so we jumped in the boat and headed upriver. We soon arrived at an elaborate tree-blind, situated in a complex, multi-fingered, channel junction and bend in the river. About five hundred decoys were out and meticulously placed to handle both traffic, and varying winds. We climbed up the ladder and I asked Ray, "who's blind is this?"

He just said, "friends."

There was a charcoal bucket, still warm, and some empty hulls in the blind. Things were looking up. A few minutes later Ray had some ducks working, but a boat was coming which scared them off. The boat pulled up and sat in front of the blind. Ray said, "Let's go," and we climbed back down the ladder into our boat, waved, and took off. Not a word was said. This scene was repeated, with some slight variation, several more times before Dad called a halt. We had just been introduced to "blind hopping" on the most heavily hunted piece of public water in the state of Arkansas. It was a quiet ride home.

That was the last time we used a real guide. We learned our way around, which blinds were good in what conditions, and which ones were used by their owners and when. An old "river-rat" by the name of Dallas Hill attached himself to my dad. Daddy tried and tried to give him the slip, but Dallas seemed to have a sixth sense about when to show up. No matter how secretive or unannounced my father tried to be, he would be greeted by the wizened little man with a big smile and a "Hi Doc, you forgot to call but I figured you might be a commin', so I rode the tram in yes'tady and just been a wait'n"– What could Dad say? Dallas seemed to have been everywhere and done everything. He had a duck call, but no reed; a gun that would "Kick an' kill at both ends!"; told stories about market gunning when "The sky was the limit!"; and about "Hoop snakes" that would grab their own tails and roll like a wagon hoop– very deadly apparently.

I will say this for Dallas, he did know his way around, and as the waters began their seasonal rise, tens of thousands of acres of flooded green timber and miles of flooded bean fields became accessible. The whole bottom was criss-crossed with logging roads, runs, and ridges. We explored, we waded, blind-hopped, and stayed out all day. It was a beautiful place, and a lot of fun, but we shot no ducks.

A few weeks into the season, I asked dad if I could bring a friend from school, Hal Patton. Hal and I had bird hunted, fished, and shot doves together quite a bit, and he knew that Hal was safe with a gun. Hal didn't have a place to go duck hunting, either, so he was very eager. We both wanted to shoot a duck very badly, and the lack of past success was no deterrent to our zeal; in fact, it seemed to only fan the flames of desire.

This started another era in the education of a duck hunter—hunting with friends. Hal and I hunted every weekend and all of Christmas vacation that year. Our normal "modus operindi" was to leave the clubhouse in the black dark, long before the other club members were about, carrying four bacon and egg sandwiches apiece- courtesy of Mrs. Hoots- and scour the globe looking for the "mother-load" of ducks. We would return about ten o-clock to pick up "Doc" and Dallas, and fill up with gas. We hunted with the grown men until they wanted to go in for lunch. After a few hamburgers, and maybe a bowl of chili or two, while the men took naps, we would go back out and hunt until dark.

We had near misses, we almost killed ducks, but we never got one. We could both call ok, and we could both shoot ok, but it takes experience to learn when to call, and more importantly, when to shoot; decoy arrangement is an art that is never fully mastered; movement and concealment require everyone to know what to do, and at exactly the right times, or you don't get a shot. It can be a very steep learning curve to master on your own.

We loved every minute of it, and to this day, neither of us would trade one of those days for any other.

One of the worst blunders we made was to move (locations) all the time. My dad used to tell people that on one weekend Hal and I burned eight, six gallon tanks of gasoline, through a fifteen horsepower Johnson outboard. On the other hand, by the end of that season I don't think there was a soul on the planet that knew those bottoms as well as we did.

It was the last day of the last weekend, before we finally broke the spell. The river had frozen over and no boats could make it up from the public access down below. We had some open water upriver, where the current was strong, and Dr. Cocke's blind was one of those places. Daddy, Chuck Berry, Hal, and I hunted there all morning but hadn't seen many ducks. We had a couple of opportunities though, and one small group slipped in and lit off my side of the blind. I lined up heads for the proverbial "skillet shot," (no remorse at all by then), and my gun went "click-click." Mr. Berry, always the practical joker, had unloaded it. If you ever hunt with me, you will see me constantly checking and rechecking my gun—evidence of a deep mental scar made that day.

Hal and I took the "grown-ups" back and were glad to be rid of them. We had our game-faces on, and we knew the time was right.

Back in the blind, it was apparent that the ducks were starting to move. I blew an Olt duck call, and Hal a Yentzen. We thought they sounded fairly good together, and a couple of bunches gave us a look in the usual, suspicious way, where never more than one at a time offered a decent shot. We decided to change the rules. No more Mr. Nice Guy; this wasn't one of those fancy, "country club" green-timber places, and if we ever got another duck in shooting range, we were going to shoot, and shoot hard—no matter how many more were right behind. On this river, it was no-holds-barred, survival of the fittest- Hatchie Coon rules.

It wasn't long before another contented flock of mallards came chattering down the river. Wow, without boat traffic this was a whole new world! They stayed high, ignoring our invitation, except for a lone "Suzie," who did one of those spectacular "kamikaze" dives, straight down, and then right back up. She was screaming fast, and only in range for a second, but the new rules were in place. A near simultaneous double-report left the front of the blind, and the suzie crumpled dead-in-the-air, and hit the water with a resounding "PLOP!"—one of the greatest sounds in all of duck hunting. Hal and I stared, thunderstruck, at each other for a moment, and then scrambled for the boat. There was a lot of current right there, but she had barely cleared the decoys by the time we got to her. Holding her up by the bill, she was passed back and forth, as we marveled at the intricate beauty and design of her perfect brown camouflage. Without a word passing between us, we knew what had to be done. Hal, gently smoothing out her beautiful plumage, laid her tenderly on the front of the boat–for all to see. I cranked the motor and headed back to the club—we HAD to show her to my dad.

This photo shows the "new" tram a few years after the time of this story. From left to right: Mr. Crutchfield (caretaker at that time), Dr. Charles L. Neely (Dad), Jack Stokes, the author, and the infamous "Dallas Hill."

The boat ditch at Hatchie Coon, seen from the club house. My dad and Mr. Hoots are in the foreground, no doubt irritated at my "wide open" boating style.

"Ole Reliable"

It was February, duck season was over, no fish were biting, and an ice storm had closed down school for several days. This was a real buster of an ice storm where every blade of grass, every tree limb, twig, power line and road was thickly covered in gleaming, clear ice.

The telephone rang and my dad, who was about to try to make it to the hospital, answered. I was in another room, but could hear, "Hello, he's right here." I sprang from the chair with all the pent-up energy of a young teenager that has been given a reprieve from school but trapped in the house for two, excruciatingly full, days. My friend and fellow outdoors devotee, Jack, was on the line and he wanted to know if I could go on a GNS with he and his dad. "Daddy, Mr. Stokes is going to take us out to North Lake Hunting Club on a GNS... OK?"

Fearful of having so much destructive energy pent-up in the house for another day, he consented readily. "Uhm Buck... what IS a GNS?"

I told him, "It stands for 'Grand Negro Safari' where we go out like the colored people in the country do and hunt any kind of game we can find but we get points for what we shoot and at the end of the day there will be a prize!"

Daddy just shook his head and said, "Be careful."

Mr. Stokes, or "Mr. John," as he later became known to me, was the instigator of these types of outings, but I don't know if he came up with the terminology; you see, Mr. John was possessed of fairly liberal views, with no semblance of racism allowed. Be that as it may, these outings were just about having some good clean fun.

One of the great things about Mr. John, as far as we young boys were concerned, was that he had a vast and embattled array of tried and true equipment. His "river boat," an old ski boat painted olive drab, was named "War Torn" and did double duty in the summer as a salt water fishing vessel. His gun, an A-5 with a "cuts-compensator" on the end, didn't have any bluing on it, a result, no doubt, of the vast numbers of shells fired through it. You see, in those days Mr. John was not one hundred percent limit conscious. I say that neither to condone nor condemn such behavior, that's just the way it was at that time, and it was more common than not. As to the "cuts compensator"; for those of you who are unsure as to its function, it was a metal device attached to the end of the barrel with slats, or grooves, on the sides. These grooves could project the sound waves resulting from the shot straight out to the sides thereby fulfilling the function of deafening anyone unfortunate enough to be standing nearby, a puzzling invention to say the least. His back-house was a treasure trove of old hunting, fishing, and camping gear, piled deep enough to provide a couple of youngsters with many a rainy day excavation. Mr. John's hunting car was one of those early model Suburbans with the old Co-op tires. The voluminous back end was always full of enough gear for any eventuality. It was solid white, dented, scratched, habitually mud covered, and the inside smelled of coffee, canvas, rubber, and dog. It was "Ole Reliable," one of the all time "greats," and one of a kind.

Jack and his Dad pulled into my driveway and slowly eased to a stop on the ice. I could barely stand up as I loaded my gun and vest in the back, and then skated around to the side door. "Think we'll make it?" I asked.

"We'll see," Mr. John, the eternal optimist said, "and I don't think there will be any traffic!"

The old North Lake Hunting Club was located just south of Memphis along the Mississippi River. Normally a twenty-minute drive, it was noon before we made it to the gate.

Mr. John set the day's rules: "Boys, this is how it's going to be; quail are three points, rabbits four, beaver fifteen, foxes and coyotes twenty, deer and turkey thirty-five. Any questions?" Jack and I wanted to know how many points blackbirds and tweety birds were. "One point for blackbirds, minus one point for tweety birds." Wow, there were penalties involved for promiscuous shooting this time; we boys started to worry about that. I wanted to know what the prize was; "A berry pie on the way home." My stomach growled at the mention of food, a reminder that the Stokes don't eat at regular times like most people, and we had just missed lunch.

Most of the club was composed of gigantic soybean fields with occasional ditches running through them. These ditches were approximately ten feet deep and twenty yards wide, full of briars, vines, and tangles. The plan was to line up, stomp through every piece of cover, and shoot anything that got up.

The first ditch that we tried had a large covey of quail on it. They flushed wild, offering no shots, and re-lit scattered along the ditch in front of us, offering good singles shooting. We bagged several, and a few rabbits along the way. The rabbits were especially challenging in the thick cover because they rarely gave us more than a split second look as they sprinted down their well-known trails and tunnels. Noticing a small tree out to the side that was covered with blackbirds, I quickly scored fifteen points in two shots, which prompted Jack to belly crawl out a feeder ditch and rake a bunch on the ground to keep us about even. When we got back to "Ole Reliable" it looked like we had enough time for one more drive. Mr. John gave it a little thought, and then said, "Load up boys, we'll ease down the levee and push the big ditch that runs all the way back into the timber. If we are lucky, there might be a few deer hiding in there."

As we drove to the new spot, it became apparent that something unusual was going on. Every deer and turkey on the place, and there were hundreds of them, was standing out in the field as far away from the timber as it could get. As we drove by, at a distance of only a few hundred yards, they didn't even run. Normally, just the sight of a vehicle at any distance would send turkeys airborne. The deer, on the other hand, were not so spooky, as this had been a shotgun-only club for quite a few years. We figured that the only explanation for this odd behavior had to be falling ice. It was a clear, sunny day, about thirty-two degrees, and the trees held tons and tons of ice, which a gentle breeze was starting to shake loose.

Small game was quickly forgotten as we re-huddled for the new plan. Jack and I were to get down in the bottom of the ditch and creep all the way to the woods and then position ourselves for a shot when the unsuspecting game headed our way. Mr. John was going to give us twenty minutes, and then he and his lab were going to slowly work their way down the ditch toward us, keeping in plain view of the quarry, and attempt to push something over us. The only chink in this plan was that neither deer nor turkey season was open, and furthermore, those woods were not part of the club. Because of this slight legal oversight, Jack and I were given strict instructions to only shoot one time apiece, no more, and then scramble back to the ditch with our bag, if anything, and hide until we were picked up. It was with great excitement that we budding young sportsmen took on the appointed task.

Upon reaching the woods, a careful reconnaissance revealed that we had somehow slipped by undetected, and that there were probably five hundred turkeys out there, only a hundred or so yards away. We both shot Remington 870 pump shotguns with eight shot magazine extensions on them, loaded all the way to the gills with #8 shot, which was all we had with us. It was with infinite care and deadly stealth that we took up our positions.

As we crouched, silent and tense, awaiting whatever was to come, ice crashed down all around us. Each time the breeze moved a branch or limb, cascades of ice would fall, striking other branches and so on, until the whole under storey was in motion. It was eerie, surreal, and definitely dangerous. Nothing happened for a while as we lay there, shielding our heads and shivering. Suddenly, a shrill whistle broke the spell, and immediately, all those turkeys went airborne, coming right at us in a giant waive. We didn't know it, but the whistle was a "come in" command, and warning. The local game warden, a real "go getter" and personal adversary of Mr. John's, had just driven down the levee and seen all those turkeys and "Ole Reliable." He knew it was Mr. John's vehicle, and, coincidently, that something was going on. He had slowly driven on by to the next off-ramp, and concealed his truck behind some trees. That was when Mr. John had whistled.

So here we were, two eager young boys, a perfectly executed plan and a perfect flush. I picked out a tremendous long-beard as it glided slowly past but he seemed to just soak up the #8 shot to little effect, requiring three more before finally crashing down on the fourth. So much for the one shot rule. Jack, from the sound of things, was having a similar experience. My prize, it turns out, was just playing possum, and led me a lively chase full of running, loading, and shooting that eventually left me with neither ammunition nor turkey to show for it. When I made it back to the scene of the crime, Jack was waiting and had a similar story of frustration. He was also in a hurry to leave because his Dad had whistled several more times—something might be wrong.

When we made it back to the ditch, Mr. John described the situation, with numerous references to "following instructions" and something about WWII. He had even killed a turkey that had fled the woods to get away from us. His rational, as explained to us had been, 'why not? Those two must have ten apiece in there by now!' Quickly, we loaded up to make a run for it, including the turkey. Though somewhat lax about seasons and bag limits, Mr. John was adamant that no game ever be wasted, even if that meant getting caught with it.

We then clawed our way out to the levee and up the side, with the help of a good bit of momentum. At the top, we turned right, headed towards freedom, and the green truck was in sight, behind, but coming up fast. Once she got going, "Ole Reliable" with her long wheelbase and well distributed weight, wasn't fishtailing as much as our pursuers light, short-bed pickup truck and we gained a little on the straight away. A steep bend was coming up fast and Mr. John took it without slowing down; he put the inside tires just off the road and centrifugal forces balanced with the gravitational force down the levee and we came through the turn beautifully. He was so excited by the success of the maneuver that he shouted "Barney Olfield!" his hands a blur as he dealt the wheel back and forth. The warden swapped ends on that turn, and slid all the way down to the base of the levee, but was not out of it. Tearing along at the base, he actually gained a little, and with several tries, and some fairly gutsy driving of his own, he performed a "run and gun" maneuver that put him back in the chase. Thirty minutes of slipping and sliding later, we were at the club gate with the warden only a minute behind us. Mr. John said, "Ok boys, you pray that gate is unlocked, and if it is, you two jump out and lock it as fast as you can." It was, and with trembling hands, we did. As Mr. John remembers it, "I drove slowly away, waving in the rearview mirror." Apparently, not everyone had a key.

At the first "Quick Stop," on Third Street, Jack and I were both declared winners and treated to a berry pie and a coke. A little overwhelmed, we ate in silence while Jack's dad regaled us with stories of daring, danger, game wardens, and events long past. Wide-eyed and attentive, we soaked it all in.

The next day school was back in, and we talked about our experience, and what we had learned. First, we needed to be more careful, and law-abiding, times were changing; second, Jack's Dad wasn't going to follow us in that direction, right away; and third, we needed to carry a few magnum loads next time, just in case.

"Mr. John" and Jack Stokes, circa 1972

A typical "GNS" bag included quail, woodcock, rabbit, and coon.

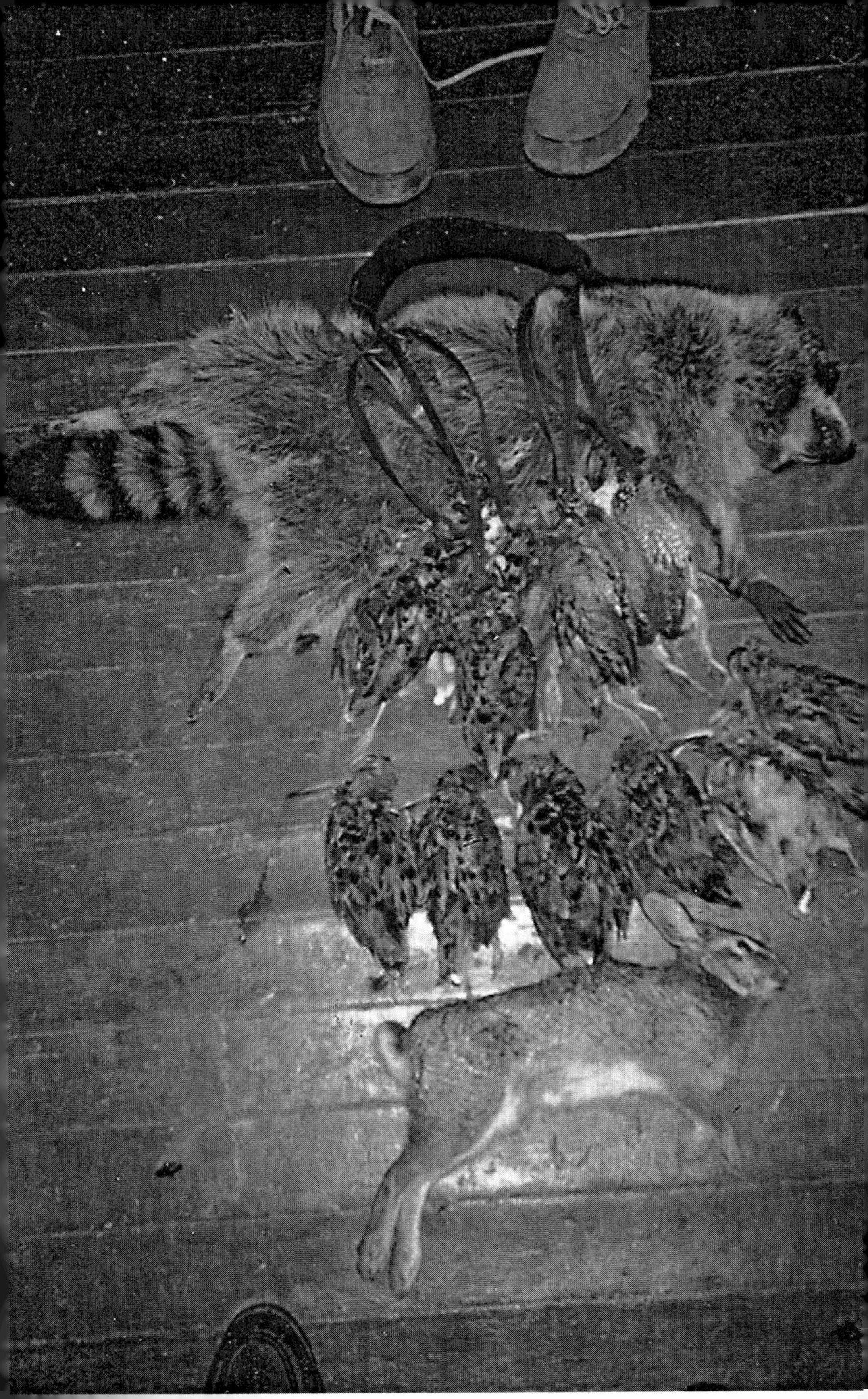

The Truman Blind

Pre-driving age summers are difficult for the aspiring outdoorsman. Parents tend to have a life of their own, and possibly even a vocation. School age boys are looking for the former, preferably exciting, and maybe a smidgeon of the latter.

My own most earnest desire in those days was to be a "river rat"– Specifically, a commercial fisherman on the St. Francis river of Arkansas. The freedom of being out on the river, in a boat, outwitting the numerous aquatic denizens, was extremely attractive, but it also got me out of Memphis, and away from parental supervision. To do this required planning, and transportation. Being a stubborn sort, and wanting to be in control of my own destiny, I was reluctant to involve my parents any more than was essential. This left only one option— the bus.

Continental Trailways left Memphis, most mornings, at seven in the morning, and could drop me off at the road going in to Tulot by ten. This left only the five mile walk to the head of the tram tracks, where I could meet the "tram"- a Volkswagon bus fitted out with railroad wheels- which then transported me across swamp and through bottomland forest, to my base of operations, the Hatchie Coon club. Seems like a lot of trouble now, but for a young fellow, it was an adventure.

In those days it was unusual for a young white boy to ride the bus at all, much less one equipped for life on the frontier. I usually carried a gun, cased, and a rod case, and a duffle bag with enough clothes, ammunition, and fishing tackle for a weeks stay. It was quite a load. The city bus would pick me up at five a.m., and make the downtown connection in plenty of time. The drivers were a little surprised to see the baggage and artillery, but invariably were only curious. This was obviously before we had terrorists, Pita, or Greenpeace; hunters were OK, and I guess I just didn't look too menacing.

On the walking leg of my journey, I passed three houses and a store; the thriving metropolis of Tulot. Situated right next to the gravel road, this store was cool, dark, and inviting, after the dust and heat, a great place to retreat for a "chocolate soldier," and to use the "party line" telephone to call Mr. Hoots for a pick-up with the tram.

This worthy, white haired, gentleman, with tobacco-stained handlebar mustache, and year-round jump-suite, was my partner in the industry. Aside from the occasional sport fishing expedition, the club received very little summer-time use. To supplement income, Mr.

Hoots ran a few nets, trotlines, and fish traps, peddling his catch from the back of his pick-up in either Truman or Jonesboro.

This was my kind of work! We, or rather, I, most of the time, ran and baited twice a day, taking our catch back to the dock and unloading into large holding pens built out in the current for aeration. Buffalo, carp, and catfish, were segregated, and usually sold on Saturdays—alive, or in tubs on ice. We split sixty-forty, and I cut the grass and worked around the club for board. Let it not be overlooked, that the way to a growing boy's heart, is through his stomach, and Mrs. Hoots was one of those wonderful country ladies who could really lay on the groceries. Luckily, as with most great cooks, she loved to see her work disappear. This was a growing period for me, four-hamburger meals for instance, and I was really in the right place.

Bait was a constant problem. The best was usually live crawfish, sometimes minnows, but later on in the summer they can be hard to find and even harder to keep alive. Another good option was live fresh water mussels. The St. Francis was full of them and they were accessible whenever the river was low. The usual method used to collect them was to get out of the boat and float along in the current, in shallow water, feeling along on the bottom with both hands. They tend to bunch up, so if you found one, there were usually hundreds within a few yards.

One hot summer day, after running my lines, I was probing about for new muscle beds and found the mother load. A triangular shaped sand bar, just outside the main channel, with a secondary channel running right behind it. The firm, sandy-clay bar, encompassed about an acre of shallow water, and had mussels from end to end. When I glanced around to get some bearings for my new bait shop, the first thing I saw was a very odd structure. Overlooking the bar was the tallest tree-blind, for duck shooting, that I had ever seen. Twenty feet above the water, and crafted into the giant cypress trees, rested a six man blind, complete with warming room, cooking gear, comfortable chairs, and everything else you can think of. A series of ladders gave access, and everything was in perfect order. These guys were serious!

Back at the clubhouse that evening, consultation with the big aerial map gave a name for this blind— The Truman Blind. Curiosity peaked; I started to gather more information. Just off of club property, no one seemed to know much about them. Mr. Hoots said that they had been there for years, were a group out of Truman, but he didn't know them personally. The club president, Scott May, said that the last time that he had hunted nearby, the occupants of the blind had exhibited a degree of proficiency and professionalism, the likes of which he had never witnessed before. "The Truman bunch are the 'A-Team' of duck shooters," he told me, "They hunt big groups, four or five good callers, hand paint every decoy, and they put out a couple of hundred. Every day, every decoy line is adjusted for river fluctuation, and Lord, can they shoot! Furthermore, one day when I was in club number 1, just south of them, I could have sworn that they were shooting in 'battle line formation'. The first six would each shoot out of his hole, duck down, and then the

'B' group would shoot over their backs. It was deadly," he sighed, "beautiful, but deadly!"

Don't know if I believed all that, but I was developing a desire to hunt out of this "tallest" of blinds. Even back in those days, I was a blind connoisseur. How did they build it? Why that way? Dimensions one way when it would have been easier another. These were all questions that would run through my head every time I encountered a new model. The ultimate test of any design was to hunt out of it, and this was one I had to try.

Hot, lazy, summer days, of channel catfish, skinny-dippin, boat racing, and Mrs. Hoots cooking, soon came to an end. School, soccer, dove shoots, and bird dogs, came in their annual progression, until finally, it was time for the big one— duck season!

The first part of the season passed without the opportunity to try out the Truman Blind. Everyday that I was present, so were they, and they usually hunted all day. I did count volleys, or the number of times that they shot at groups of ducks, when possible, and it became apparent that they shot as much, or more, as any other blind on the river. Granted, on a given day the "Suck Hole" might do better, or "Bagley's Blind" at times, but day in and day out they were just as good.

Over time, I noticed a few tricks they were using. The brush job was innovative. Composed entirely of honey-suckle vines, it extended over the entire blind about a foot thick, cascading down the front 10-15 feet below the structure itself. The effect was to hide this massive structure inside an even more massive thicket, so that it just disappeared.

The decoys were unusual also. Hard plastic magnums with bright, light green heads, and large, blue and white wing patches, all meticulously hand painted and shellacked to shine. The effect was bright and flashy, but mimicked no species on the Mississippi flyway, or any other for that matter. They used full bricks for anchors, and heavy cord— surprisingly all-white cord– that was wound around the decoys necks as the river rose and fell. This straight up-and-down anchoring system eliminated the incessant tangling that most other blinds had to contend with.

The shooting holes were completely perpendicular, with the roofline coming all the way over the shooters head, like trying to shoot out of an upstairs window. This configuration completely eliminated any chance of taking a straight up shot, but it did make it possible for the callers/shooters to stand in complete shadow, and look right at the birds as they were working out over open water. With tall timber behind, and half a mile of open water in front, it was a good set-up.

As the season progressed, the river rose, and flooded the big timber bottoms. This was my favorite type of duck hunting, and all the un-crowded room in the world to do it in. My dad and I, and sometimes a friend, traveled far and wide from the clubhouse in our pointed duck boat. We were happy to spend sunlit days tracking the whereabouts of large concentrations of mallards that moved constantly, following the river's crest and the availability of new flooded bottomland. Drakes only, was the rule, and no shots taken below the trees. A call, a gun, and waders, were all the equipment needed, and maybe some of Mrs. Hoots sandwiches in the boat.

Over Christmas, a two-day mandatory enforced break in duck shooting, a big storm hit the mid-south. Arctic temperatures froze all the slack water, and what ducks didn't leave, hit the rivers. I was frantic to get back to the club, and dad agreed to go Christmas night, and let me bring a friend, for a five-day hunt. I immediately called up Hal Patton, and the hunt was on.

When we got to the club, the boat ditch was frozen thick, as were the woods, but the main channel was still open. Forecasts were for single digits the next couple of nights, and the worry was the river might freeze completely over. The only hunting possible this week would be the river blinds near the channel that had good current.

Several members were present for the draw that evening. A ritual affair, the draw had been held at seven o'clock in the evening, for the next day's shoot, since the club was founded in 1884. My dad got the "Woods Blind," a good pick, and the new member, a Mr. Bobby Weaver, and his son, Robert, chose the "Alabama Blind." We made a deal where we would team up, if the shooting sounded better at the others blind. Sleep was difficult for us youngsters, as it always was on the first night of a trip. I would lay in bed, with eyes tightly shut, and be certain that I was never going to go to sleep, then be startled from a deep sleep, by the "wake up knock" on the door.

Next morning, after we had broken a trail to the river, dad and I headed north, to our blind. Mr. Weaver encountered heavy ice trying to go south, and had to turn around. This was both good and bad. Bad, because they couldn't make it to the Alabama Blind, but good because public access to the river was cut off. We had the whole river to ourselves. Taking a cruise up the unusually quiet river, the Weavers noticed the unoccupied Truman Blind, and decided to give it a try.

With no competition, the Weavers finished their hunt with great success, as did we. By chance, we met them on the river on our way back, and we both stopped and drifted down the river together. After sharing our hunting stories, and the grown-ups having a toast or two, it was time to head back to the club for one of Mrs. Hoots fabulous meals. I couldn't help noticing that the Weavers had a bag of charcoal in their boat, but no charcoal bucket. Thinking that it might have been left behind, I brought it to their attention. Mr. Weaver said that they had just used the one in the blind.

The next morning it was not as cold as had been predicted. Open water lanes had apparently appeared overnight, and several boats had already gone by the club, heading north. Dad, Hal, and I got a late start, and it was full daylight when we passed the Truman Blind—or at least where it had been. Some charred bark, and a few smoking board ends, were all that remained.

Now, blind wars were common on the St. Francis at that time. People were always trying to encroach on the best holes and if you didn't shove back, you ended up getting crowded out. But the Truman Blind didn't encroach on anybody but us, and we didn't burn it… intentionally anyway. Charcoal buckets can get cherry-red-hot.

Whatever the cause, the Truman boys were not about to lose their spot. An absolute flotilla of industry, they had it built back, by the end of the day, AND BRUSHED! Where they came up with that much honeysuckle, in late December, is beyond me.

That night, the predicted cold air mass moved in and the river iced over again. The whole bottom was eerily quiet, with just the cracks and pops of a frozen landscape. Dad elected to stay by the fire and Hal and I worked at getting the boat out of the ditch, and closer to the somewhat thinner ice of the river. It was a chore, and took us an hour or two, but we had a large, heavy, V-bottom boat, nicknamed "The Tank," and a lot of willpower. The technique was to push the bow up on the ice using the motor, run to the front and jump up and down until it broke through, then run back and repeat the process. It was also a good way to keep warm.

Out in the current the ice was much thinner. Open leads of water came and went, with maybe ½ inch thick ice between them. We decided to "ride an look," as far as we could go, and, as a rule when conditions were bad, Dad wanted us to head upstream, in case of motor trouble.

Heading north, we saw very few ducks. They were either not around, or we were making so much noise breaking ice that they left far in advance. A few got up from the Truman Blind decoys, where we encountered a long stretch of open water. Taking this a couple of miles brought us to the islands of "Fish Head," a famous shooting spot with several blinds owned by the James family, who guided in the area. They were not there that day, and as we rounded the first island several hundred Canadian geese, tightly packed into a small pocket of open water, irrupted in front of the boat. Our momentum carried us right into the middle of the bunch, and Hal, who was up front, and loaded (our custom at that time), fired both barrels into the only two tiny little holes in the entire sky, that did not have geese in them. My gun, zipped up in a case, and shells in an unopened box, even had time to shoot a straggler. We almost never had opportunities at geese, in those days, and Hal still thinks about those misses I'm sure.

That was about the end of the open water, and so we turned the boat around, and headed for the Truman Blind to sit it out. The newly refurbished blind was exactly like the old one. The boat was tied up at the base of the first ladder, and gear was passed up in stages. Inside, was the same warming room, though this time the charcoal bucket rested on a bed of sand, and the shooting porch had the same design.

We took up our positions, calling occasionally, and enjoyed the elevated view on that brilliantly bright, cold, clear day.

It was not the kind of day when one sees a lot of ducks. Most had moved on south, or were sitting tight. It *was* the type of day when just about everything that came by, came in. Usually, the first warning we would have of impending action was the jet engine-like sound of rushing wings, loosing altitude fast, and from a very great height. It was one of those rare days, rare in that area of mostly mallard shooting, when almost every kind of duck that we had ever seen on a chart, came into the decoys. Teal, widgeon, gadwall, black duck, and spoonbill, were added to our goose, along with pintail, and mallard. We managed to bag one or two of each species, and the shot opportunities were just often enough to be pleasant, but not frantic. We had time to admire each species, in full plumage, and speculate as to why it was built the way it was.

Early in the afternoon a boat could be heard, far to the South, breaking ice and trying to come up river. The acoustics were such that we thought it might be five miles down river, or more. Thirty minutes later it was still in heavy ice but a good bit closer. This was discouraging for us because it was so noisy that there was little possibility of our getting a shot, and if they kept coming, the disturbance was going to be with us for a long time. Soon, the boat hit some open water, which we reckoned was just south of the club. A few minutes later, the honking of geese could be heard, and then a loud—Boom! There was total silence after that. The boom had sounded like a shot, but a little odd, and the motor had quit, or at least we never heard it anymore. Puzzled, we speculated as to what had happened to the boat for a few minutes, and since we were about done anyway, it was decided to head back to the fire and hot food.

That evening, as the grownups had cocktails and told stories of other "ice out" hunting experiences, the tram could be heard approaching, and Hal and I went out to see who had come. Mr. Hoots was alone this time, and looked a little depressed. He told us that a couple of local boys he knew had been out riding on the river that day, when a bunch of ducks got up in front of the boat, and the guy in back had shot the guy in front, right in the back of the head. The two boys had been brothers, and Hal and I knew them slightly. We both just looked at each other, remembering the events of the day. I don't believe we ever traveled with loaded guns again.

Mr. Hoots, teaching the author how to Skin a squirrel.

The Bayou

The Bayou De View is part of a multi-tiered drainage system that runs through the fabled duck lands of North East Arkansas. Formerly a river, channelization projects aimed at the Corps of Engineers mantra that "No stream shall flow unaltered to the sea," have decreased its flow, during dry periods, to a chain of stagnant lakes.

The headwaters start in fertile farmlands South and West of Jonesboro Arkansas, broaden into the Bayou De View State WMA, re-concentrate for bank to bank agriculture until North of Mcrory, and then broaden once more into multi-fingered bottomland flows all the way to it's junction with the Cash River at Dagmar WMA. The contiguous old-growth bottomland portion runs from just North of highway 64 almost to Clarendon, a distance of approximately fifty-five miles, where the Cash then joins the White River and begins a seventy-mile run to the Mississippi.

The three drainages, commonly subject to extensive flooding and therefore never cleared, create the largest remaining contiguous natural bottomland hardwood forest in North America.

Much of the land remains private but all three drainages contain large tracts of public land. The aforementioned Bayou De View WMA, Dagmar WMA, Watensaw State Game Area, the gigantic White River National Wildlife Refuge and Trusten Holder State WMA, will all remain pristine for eternity.

I have had the opportunity to visit most of these bottomlands over the last few decades. During summer months the fishing can be good for a variety of river dwelling species. With proper water levels, the duck shooting can be about as good as it gets, but what really brings me back to the Bayou, year after year, is the trees; Bald Cyprus specifically. This species, widespread over a vast range, reaches its apex here. Sunlight, temperature, timing of overflows, parturition, and the necessary fertility of soil, all come together to produce the behemoths of the world.

The bases of some of these specimens are wider than a sixteen foot boat and have virtual forests of knees around them, with many grown tall and seemingly welded together into strange shapes and structures. Ancient compared to local civilization, all of them are hollow, or partly so. Most have their crowns blasted off by centuries of lightning and tornadoes. It is not uncommon for the top of the trunk to be four feet in diameter at its peak.

Whitetail deer of great age and wisdom are found there, and the hounds have a hard time of it, in winter, because of all the islands and ridges. Fox squirrels are common, with an occasional melanistic to be seen, as are a multitude of the usual furbearers, including black bear. Cottonmouths are king of the reptilians and the insect world probably has endemics new to taxonomy by legion. The bird life is strictly southern, with the migrants that follow drainages abundant. Recently, the once extinct Ivory Billed woodpecker has been "discovered," not surprising due to the age and cavity prone structure of the forest.

Having hunted this area for many years, the discovery of the Ivory Bill got me thinking. Shadowy memories of rounding a bend in the boat; Dark figures in swooping flight—unusual markings. Another time; tree topping mallards in the bright sun of a clear- cold day and in between flights—glimpses of a dark shape, scooting up the bowl of a big cypress...unusually large.. a different species... maybe.

I did not carry a "Petersons Guide" with me in those days but I did love the outdoors, and I did notice things. There were other memories, some less defined, until I went way back, and a cold realization swept through me— I may have even held one.

We were about 14, Hal and I, when his dad joined the old "Lucky 13" hunting club near Hunter, Arkansas. The land was leased from a local farmer, and included rice fields, sloughs, and several miles of the Bayou De View. All the fields bordering the Bayou had been in rice, and the harvest season had been wet. The roads were absolutely horrible. Imagine four-wheel drive tractors, four-wheel drive combines, semi-trucks filled with rice, and then place them all in a greasy-gumbo-mud rice field with one dirt road in or out...then let it rain a few more times.

Mr. Patton did not have a four-wheel drive vehicle at that time. His hunting car was a "Travel All," which I believe was made by International, whenever they were in the car business (not long obviously), and he was quick to exclaim— "but I've got pozy traction!" Well, Hal and I didn't have anything but boots, so we were ecstatic to jump in—positive traction and all.

There were two things that quickly became apparent: 1) positive traction works better when pushed from behind, 2) positive traction is aided by momentum…lots of momentum. Because Hal and I were both small and scrawny, Mr. Patton became adept at the development of momentum. It is quite possible that International knew what they were about, in the car making business, because that Travel All was subjected to a lot of the same maneuvers that one would see on the popular television show "The Dukes of Hazard," and it held up! I think the thing nearly floated and was impossible to drown out.

Even so, due to travel limitations, many of our hunts ended up on foot, and there came a time when the only option was to begin that way. Distance and water negated the attempt, and Hal and I walked down the gravel road to the farmer's grain bins, to try and shoot a few doves. There were lots of doves, and quite a few black birds, feeding on spilt rice, and our shooting woke up the farmer's son, Keith.

Keith was a curly haired redhead, a few years older than us, and had "been out late," apparently, and talked about a lot of things that we didn't know much about. I think his attention was on beer, and girls, both very interesting of course, but the real important fact was that he had a truck— a four-wheel drive truck.

Keith lived a long way away from anyone else, and was not hard to manipulate. He was to pick us up for the afternoon hunt, and he said that he "knew a place."

We were ready at noon, but it was late afternoon before he showed up. The truck was a Chevy, and was equipped with something called a "short block 400," "headers," and best of all— tall Co-op mud grips. We literally flew through areas heretofore impassable.

When Keith finally reigned in the steaming monster it was at a little weedy slash full of dead trees and water. The plan, as explained by our guide, was to "spread out and wait." There were no ducks in sight and only a few minutes of shooting light left. Resigned to our fate, Hal and I hiked to the other end and took up positions. With no decoys, and no blind, it was a simple procedure.

There were a few doves flying around, and Keith shot a few times, but at what we could not tell. At dark, Hal and I met up on the bank to hike back. That's when the ducks started coming. Waive after waive they poured into the deadening and fire irrupted from our host's gun in a steady stream.

Perhaps the phenomena of sound should be mentioned here. As I am sure you are perfectly aware, guns are a lot louder at night. Especially when you are not supposed to be shooting them. When a member of your party fires one, well after legal shooting time, it seems certain that every household in the county must be not only aware of it, but able to instantly pinpoint its location. This is the first thought that comes to every member of the party that is not doing the shooting. The non-shooters have several different choices they can make at this time and there are numerous pros and cons to be weighed. I'm sure you can guess which one we made. Alas, back to the story.

It was, of course, a wood duck roost and you could not scare them away. Being young, impressionable, and eager, we soon had our limits and were back at the truck. Even Keith quit shooting eventually, as Hal and I stood in the dark and listened to all the wings and whistles, saw occasional glimpses of dark bodies, and heard the splashes as they plopped down on the water.

Woodies make a lot of different noises. They yodel, whistle, half yodel, and keen. All are descriptive terms that don't come close to what they do; bottom line is, they are noisy, in a musical way, and if you put a few thousand in a small place, it is something to hear.

Keith eventually loomed in the darkness nearby with both hands full of ducks.

"Are they all woodies?" asked Hal.

"Mostly," answered our host, "and a big funny looking bird." Curious, I reached over the side of the truck and pawed through the pile of ducks in the back. In the dark, I located the odd bird. Large, differently shaped, obviously a woodpecker of some sort, I was holding it by the bill, and was fairly certain that it was unfamiliar, but, I did not make a habit of shooting a lot of woodpeckers. Oddly enough, even through the mists of time, I am almost certain the bill was white.

That was many years ago, and, at that time, the Ivory Bill was extinct. I don't know if one can get in trouble for shooting something that doesn't exist or not, but I do think that was one, because the sightings have all been very close to that exact spot. I also don't know if they ate him or not. Keith's family soon moved away and the state bought the property. We now access the area by boat, and keep a sharp lookout for the big birds.

Neither I, nor anyone else that I am aware of, have seen one since the original, "somewhat confirmed," sighting. I hope they can make a comeback.

Hal Patton, circa 1974

Steel

It was just after Christmas of a fairly uneventful waterfowl season when the tram brought me up to the clubhouse mound at old Hatchie Coon. I was alone, dad being on call at the hospital, and Continental Trailways had been happy to give me a lift, guns and all. School holidays, you see, were meant to be used to the fullest. My hunting efforts up to date had been spent at other places, and a quick look at the logbook affirmed why. Other than opening weekend, very few ducks had been killed and river conditions remained low throughout the period. Nostalgia had bought me back here, not expectations of a banner shoot, so I was content to walk about the old club and soak up the "feel" of it.

I carried my bag into a room in the "men's wing" and began to organize my gear. The old familiar "Duxbak" canvas pants, wool socks that came up above the knee if you wanted them to, a battered "pork-pie" canvas hat, an old style Olt call with a very few coveted "bands" on it, and the all important duofold union suit, were all laid out in order to be donned in the early morrow.

Next came the traditional visual inspection of boat dock, lockers, and river stage. As reported, the beloved St. Francis was well within her banks, which meant zero chance of a woods shoot tomorrow. Standing on the elevated walkway overlooking the river, a steady west wind seemed to be building up, and it had a bite to it. A feeling, not born of the wind, caused an elevation in pulse rate, and my eyes swung involuntarily to the sky. Things were looking up.

After bailing out the big V-hull, gassing up, and loading shell bucket, charcoal bucket, cushions and paddle, the sound of the tram clattering back home drew me to the clubhouse.

The old bus was unusually full, and disgorged 3 members, all with guests, and another member's son. The son was Edward Pidgeon and I was extremely glad to see him.

Club rules stated that members' sons could hunt, up to a certain age, but not participate in the draw for blinds. With three members present, and possibly more to come, we were going to get the dregs, no ifs, ands, or buts about it.

Edward is whom they were thinking of when they came up with the term "AVID." Weaned on a black Olt duck call and brought up in the rough and tumble waterfowling world of the St. Francis Sunken Lands, he was the perfect partner for the situation at hand.

We immediately started to "strategize." Picking up his bag from the platform, Edward said in a low, conspiratorial tone "West, isn't it?"

"Yeah," I answered, "maybe a little North, it's getting colder."

He stood still a minute, thinking, "Cocke's Blind?"

"Yep," I answered.

"But they won't pick it?"

"No chance, they'll go to the project. No body's been in there for a week and there are a few ducks using it. Besides, the rivers been up and down a couple of feet and the decoys out there will be all messed up."

Thinking a minute, Edward said what we both knew but didn't want to admit, "We'll have to compete with the 'Suck Hole'."

"Yeah… we will."

The "Suck Hole" was a commercial guide's blind that was operated by O.J. James. Situated on what was, arguably, the best spot on the river, it had been in operation for several generations of James's, including some during market gunning days. The James's knew how to hunt their spot, did so every day and in all conditions, and were a force to be reckoned with. O. J. was rumored to be able to read the ducks minds, and, after spending many a duckless day, watching the "Suck Hole" pounding away, all day long, I could believe it.

As we walked down the dock to look at the river again, I noticed a huge stack of decoys, hundreds of them, and all rigged with half-bricks and heavy line for the river. As yet undeployed, their potential struck me as the answer to our predicament. When I stopped, Edward followed my gaze.

"They won't all fit in the boat," he said.

Mind racing with newfound possibilities, I answered, "We can take two boats, and make several trips."

A big grin was starting to spread over both of our faces when he took a deep breath and said, "It just might work."

Edward's boat was made ready in a jiffy but the actual loading was postponed until after the draw, which took place at seven p.m. We had to be sure that "Cocke's" blind was ours, and we also needed darkness. No one needed to know what we were up to, or we might lose the fruit of our labor.

It was with carefully concealed excitement that we went into the clubhouse at the dinner bell. Mrs. Hoots, the club cook, as usual had outdone herself. On Fridays, she had fried chicken, mashed potatoes and gravy, green beans and purple hull peas put up from her copious garden, big, fluffy, cat-head biscuits, and a 4 inch thick layered chocolate sheet cake. Edward, a diabetic, had to take another shot to finish, but we "tucked in" as only hungry teenagers can do, in anticipation of an active night.

During the draw, held after dinner, only one member chose the river, and he picked "Bagley's Blind." We were free and clear to get to work.

The stars were bright and a heavy frost covered the metal surfaces when we finished loading the two boats. The weight of the bricks limited our carrying capacity to about one hundred and fifty blocks/boat, so the plan was to make two trips. A mile run upriver, through the familiar stump field and past the scattered mudbars, brought us to a sharp, ninety-degree bend with a huge open water pocket, carved out by the relentless current. Tucked into the willows, on the South side, the inside bend, was a standard four-man floating blind on

Cyprus logs. As was customary on the St. Francis, there was no boat hide. One just tied up at the back door and let the boat float behind. Surprisingly, it seemed to work just fine.

This was our destination, Dr. Ed Cocke's blind. Facing north, the pocket we had to work with was probably two hundred yards across and three hundred long. It was bounded on the South by the steep bend in the river, and to the North by a willow island of about ten acres in extent. On the North end of this Island was a big, circular hole, about one hundred yards in diameter, containing a long, low, eight man floating blind. This, the infamous "Suck Hole," was our chosen opponent.

We started up-current, letting the boats drift, and began to fill in this gigantic pocket with decoys. The stars twinkled brightly and from high above, the occasional chatter of migrants drifted down as if telling us to hurry, the following would be a day of days. After the third trip, probably somewhere around eight hudred decoys later, we called a halt. It was one o'clock in the morning, and we had done all we could do. Our pocket looked like Wapanocca Federal Wildlife Refuge with one little open trail that meandered through about thirty yards from the blind. Wind, weather, and set were as good as we could ask for, and now it was up to the hunt gods of tomorrow.

Next morning, up an hour and a half before daylight, my boat was re-loaded with all essential gear. Sandwiches, shell buckets, charcoal buckets etc., everything was checked and re-checked in expectation of what might be an all-day hunt. My shell bucket seemed a little bit light, and I opened it up to take a look. Yep, it was full. Probably enough shells to last a week—I knew better than to run out. The problem was that these were not my usual 1 5/8 oz, copper coated 4's. They were "steel shot."

Bleeding heart "PETA" moms that live their entire lives without ever observing wild ducks or lifting a finger in habitat work, had apparently stormed the Capital and forced the decision that we should all shoot steel shot at waterfowl so that no duck would die from ingesting lead. Now, if it's a problem, I'm all for anything that is good for waterfowl, but I don't see how any duck is going to ingest a lead pellet in a deep, open water set-up, with no food on the bottom.

Be that as it may, the USF+WS, in their infinite wisdom, had decided to do a "test" on steel shot, and guess what, Hatchie Coon was in the test county.

Neither Edward nor I had ever shot any, but it was the law of the land, so that's what we had. It was expensive stuff too, 1 ¼ oz of 4's, sold by Winchester, was all that either one of us could find, and it sold for about twice what lead cost.

We both jumped in my boat and headed upriver well before shooting time. Several boats came by after we had entered our blind, and we heard the comments made when they rounded the bend and saw our spread. It was impressive. The James's showed up a little later in two boats, and we heard a sharp whistle from O.J., as he navigated through our pathway.

River duck shooting generally starts about mid-morning and stays good until two. The key is to be there when the flurries happen and don't get discouraged—they're coming. We both knew this, consequently the lack of early morning activity did not dampen our spirits in the least. About ten o'clock, the breeze started to freshen a bit, and some high ducks started to move. In a big, open water set-up like this, sometimes you can work these high bunches with a lot of loud volume calling. We jokingly refer to this method as the "Broad Waters Power call", but it works in some other places also, such as Reelfoot Lake, and I'm sure others. It doesn't sound much like ducks to me, but we weren't out to win any contests.

As the distant skeins road the upper winds on by, a bunch of widgeon pealed out of formation and dove for the "Suck Hole." We cranked up the volume again, got them to bank our way, coast over the spread into the perfect wind, and line up, hovering, in front of the blind. It was perfect, absolutely perfect, and you don't get many chances like that on the St. Francis.

The ensuing volley, though administered wholeheartedly, and with determination, netted exactly two handfuls of feathers. The next bunch were mallards, about forty yards out, and more feathers. I was getting suspicious. Neither Edward nor I were virgins at missing ducks, but this didn't feel right. We soon had a bunch in fairly close, and I could visibly see the pellet strikes, and had to watch the birds struggle off, limping, so to speak.

That was the day we shut down the "Suck Hole." It had never been done before. The birds flew great; they worked beautifully, the sky, a brilliant blue, showed off their colors. The species diversity was amazing. We had every species of anatidae in Arkansas give us a look. We shot, loaded, power-called, and shot some more. We tried everything we could think of, but when the eighth box of shells was empty we quit. Not a duck died cleanly from whatever was in those shells. I can guarantee that many died later on, slowly, needlessly, far more than would ever have died from ingesting lead shot. I wish our omnipotent policy makers, or a few Peta moms, could have been there.

Edward and I made a pact that day, based on moral values, instead of the law. We would not shoot any more steel shot. Until they came up with something that worked, we were outlaws. It was the right thing to do.

Over time, years of time, the shot shell manufacturers gradually started making functional steel shells. My guess is that other people had the same experience that we did, that long gone day on the St. Francis.

Nowadays we have a variety of steel shot loads that perform fairly well and a host of other non-toxic shot types to choose from. The mentality seems to be to go bigger, and faster, to make up for the inadequacies of steel as a shot choice. Some of these shells get fairly pricey. If you want to be able to kill ducks as cleanly, and at the distances that the old lead shells would, you are going to have to pay.

Being that this is a subject that interests me immensely, I have done extensive pattern testing of most of these new materials. Without naming any particular manufacturer, let me tell you what I have found to hold true with all brands.

First, and don't crucify me for saying this, I'm just reporting what I see, with hard shot, choke isn't all that big of a deal. A little less is a little better, sometimes, but all in all it doesn't affect pattern that much.

Second, slower pellets pattern better. There is obviously a point at which lethality becomes an issue, but steel 1's at 1200 feet per second will kill a duck clean at fifty yards when well hit. My advice, if anyone were to ask, would be to shoot steel shells of at or near the same speed as the target shells you practice with.

Third, and this is a no-brainer, the more pellets the denser the pattern.

Fourth, round pellets of uniform size, not over choked at the muzzle, pattern best. Some of these newer shot types come in odd shapes and sizes. Some of these pellets tend to catch some air, and slice outside the main pattern. Others, with the small pellets mixed in, though they make a hole in paper, have questionable value to me.

Having said all that, I will admit that some of the best shots I know shoot some odd shaped and super fast shells. There's no substitute for a steady hand and a sharp eye. Whatever you decide to shoot, you will have more confidence in it, and consequently shoot better, if you pattern it first.

I will say that I miss the good old days, when shotgun shell choices were simple, effective, and comparatively cheap. Maybe the amo companies did this to us?

Heroes and outlaws

There came a day in April with the bright spring sun spreading warmth to the land and causing the flora and fauna to ramp into spring's riotous mêlée, that two young men, would be sportsmen no less, decided to try their hand at turkey hunting. One of the nimrods, me, had an old, beat-up pickup truck and a fourteen foot jon boat that would fit on the ladder rack. The other boy, Jack, had a dad who was a "Master" turkey hunter and had thereby gained some vocal instruction on turkey hunting, mostly in the form of "tall tales." What we lacked in know-how was made up for with pure determination.

At that time the Eastern Wild Turkey was just making a big comeback. Decimated nation-wide by the early to mid 1900's, it is thought that their downfall can be attributed to either over-harvest by a much more rural population, or the great chestnut blight. For those of you who are not familiar with the American Chestnut, it is probably because there aren't any anymore. North America's most prominent mast producing forest species went completely extinct, over a period of only twenty years, ending in 1940. The turkeys' downfall was probably a combination of both factors, but through relocation efforts, the 1970's had decent populations and people were starting to hunt them again.

One area where they were never killed out was the Mississippi River bottomlands. Miles upon miles of contiguous habitat protected from human intrusion by floods, mosquitoes, and inaccessibility. This area served as the seed source for game and fish departments both East and South, and if you hunt Meleagris Gallopavo today, they probably came from there.

Jack and I didn't have access to turkey hunting land, and, because we were do-it yourselfers, the river seemed the obvious choice. Duck hunting was done on the river, even if only by a select few, and it appeared to us that lands up and down the river must be quasi-public, as long as you didn't go too far inland or make a nuisance of yourself. Remember, this was early on, and we hadn't fully worked out a set of legality-morality rules yet.

It was a Friday afternoon, after school, that we headed west, boat on top, to do some scouting. The river was up, probably over thirty feet on the Memphis gauge, and our target put-in spot was just across the old bridge and right off the side of the interstate. Pushed for time, and with the sun in my eyes, I missed a yellow light by a full second. As luck would have it, a Memphis Police Department black and white was also waiting at the light, preparing to turn on to my street. Jack peered intently through the back window, "He's turning!," then, "Lights are on!." Possessed of excellent reflexes, a good lead, and no sense, I hung a quick right into a low rent housing complex, followed by several more rights and lefts. Dead end! Well, we could just hide here for a few minutes; he wasn't going to be able to find us anyway. Right then, a large group of small children, up and coming model citizens no less, ran out into the street a hundred or so yards behind us. In the rearview mirror, it looked like they were all gesturing in our direction. Ever so slowly, the cruiser pulled up and blocked the street behind us.

It was thirty minutes later when, relieved, we were headed across the bridge. It probably helped that it was "formal attire" at our school on Fridays and we both still had on our ties; or it might have been that we were to scared to try to lie to the officers; or maybe they were glad to see teenagers that weren't doing something worse. At any rate they let us go with a stern warning and a last "Good luck with the turkeys!"

We put the boat in, screwed an old, used thirty-five horse power Johnson on the back, and headed into the current. The motor acquisition had been a "great deal" but it was too big for the boat and badly over-weighted the back end. This made for some tricky handling techniques to keep us afloat— but what speed! Suffice it to say that we were young, agile, and good swimmers.

The first stop was Presidents Island, a mostly industrial area south of town but with a few patches of woods in inaccessible areas. We found a few tracks, a little scratching, and a ridge-draw-ridge-draw topography that was going to necessitate a tremendous amount of wading and/or swimming to get anywhere. Perfect, we would be back at daylight and hopefully hear one gobble!

The river was like glass after sunset as we sped the five or so miles back to our landing. On a whim, we decided to cut through the flooded woods over on the Arkansas side, and see if there was any land showing at another spot we knew about. The moon was up and cast ample illumination for navigation and a damp, pervading chill settled into the air. There was no land to be found anywhere. Silhouetted in the tops of the trees a few forlorn turkeys could be seen but they had nowhere to go and we didn't bother them. Finding an old logging road that seemed headed in the right direction, I pointed the bow down it and weaved a way through flooded timber.

Nearly a mile from the highway, and still deep in the woods, we spotted a flickering light in the distance. I turned the boat to investigate and as we drew nearer, it appeared to be coming from the top of a very tall tree. This was a little unnerving. We didn't know much about other parts of the country, but around here, this was unnatural. A little closer and huge, dark, forms could be seen, high up, and scattered about in a couple of different trees. They were men. Five great big, bearded, potbellied, hairy men, buck naked, in the tops of the trees, waving and hollering. A rope hung down from the limb of one of the trees and was attached to the tip of a sunken boat.

I circled wide, to take in the situation. They were obviously, and understandably, desperate. They told us that they had burned all of their clothing and that we had seen the flame from their last boat cushion, which was comforting, as it explained the nakedness factor. There was no way that we could carry them all and it looked like they were ready to jump out on us if we got too close.

Jack and I discussed options. No one was going to come by there in the next week, much less that night. We had to get them out, but we couldn't let them touch our tippy little boat, or we would all end up in those trees.

We came up with a plan. From a distance, we told them that we would tow their boat to land, get the water out, and come back for them. Carefully, I eased the bow up to the rope and Jack untied it while I, one hand on the throttle, kept a wary eye on the "Deliverance" group. It took quite a while to drag the sunken boat out, and then back, and in the meantime, the moon had set. We loaded the whole crew into their boat, and started the long, slow, drag, through the woods. Finally, coming out into the open field we could see headlights whizzing back and forth on the interstate. Our passengers were exuberant, but I was low on gas, and the current out in the open was tough. The only choice was to crab across, with no control over where we intersected the highway. As our flotilla approached the busy road, I yelled over the motor that we could get them to land, but that was all we could do, we were parked way down the road and I was about out of gas. The leader, who sat in the front of the boat and charitably could have been described as a double to the rock star "Meatloaf," said, "I may be a big, fat, ugly, bastard, but you boys get me to land and I'm gonna kiss you!"

Jack and I looked at each other in silent communication, and just before the bow touched the berm of the highway, he cast off the rope and we sped away into the darkness—heroes for a day.

The next morning found us on the island somewhat after daylight. The ridges in this area run parallel to the river and are usually narrow, with deep draws in between. All the draws were full of water, some wadeable, others not. We stayed together, moving slow and calling often— no answer. After crossing several of these draws, we could see the light of some sort of opening, possibly a field, up ahead. A careful stalk in that direction confirmed it to be a bean field, with amazingly, a flock of turkeys pecking around out in the middle. A large gobbler, beard dragging the ground and feathers erect, strutted back and forth for his admiring harem. Alternately crawling and slithering, we got as close as possible and set ourselves up to call this big rascal in. Jack, using a "Big Turk Jake Yelper," made soothing clucks that sounded better than the tape we had listened to, while I made plaintive yelps on a home made mouth call. The gobbler liked neither, and was content to stay where he was. After an hour or so, when the flock was at the far end of the field, Jack did a risky belly-crawl out to the very edge of cover, while I stayed back in the woods and continued with the occasional yelps to no avail. Eventually, after what always seems like an eternity in these situations, the flock had slowly fed their way back down the middle of the field, and was passing by Jack's hiding place at a distance of maybe fifty yards. With an all-or-nothing attitude, Jack took the shot, and immediately followed up with another, for insurance. He was there in an instant, and promptly grabbed his prize and received a beating like I have never seen since, but hold on he did. He had his first turkey, a giant gobbler, and the first one either of us had ever seen up close!

Elated, we left at once, vowing to return early enough the next morning to hear a gobble from the roost.

The next morning was cloudy, and still, threatening rain. We split up, Jack heading north, and I to the south, along the riverbank. When I had traveled only a hundred yards or so from the boat, I began to hear gobbling, and lots of it. It sounded like fifty turkeys, to my untrained ear, and I sat down right in the middle of them and began to call. As so often happens, they all flew down together, and on the next ridge over. Keeping low, I crossed the water and made it to their ridge, and then slithered to the top in order to be able to shoot all of the width of the ridge. It would just be a matter of time before something came up or down, and I would be in range. My first tentative call brought an explosive gobble from the ridge I had just vacated. Hens started cackling, more toms gobbled, both in front and right behind me, surely in range if I could just see them, and several turkeys launched into the air and lit in the tree directly over my head. A big, fat one stood swaying on a wobbly limb, with a long beard hanging straight down. "Wham!" Down he came, and I raced to my prize, scattering hens and gobblers both along the way. The turkey fell in the water, and was doing a good bit of splashing around when I grabbed her by the neck... HER. It was a hen! Only someone who has done this can truly understand how terrible you feel at that moment.

After a few minutes worth of self-reproach, I picked up the turkey and headed for the boat. Just after crossing the last bit of water between me and the ridge where the boat was parked– I saw a man up ahead, and he was coming in my direction, and it wasn't Jack. Instinctively, I dropped the turkey and stepped behind a tree. From this observation point it did not appear that he had seen me, but on his current course he could not fail to do so. It seemed prudent to distance myself from the turkey, and I stepped out and made my way to meet this person. The Warden, the same Warden, the Warden that Jack and I had locked behind the gate some years ago, stopped and appraised my soaked and feather studded visage.

He asked me where the turkey was, and I went and got it for him. Without saying a word, he started searching around in the breast feathers, and I, looking down at my sodden boots, and feeling about as low as one can get, said, "It's a hen."

On the way back to the boat, I told him the complete story, how it was an accident, and how I didn't mean to shoot a hen. He didn't say much. Upon our arrival, Jack was seated on the bow of another boat, looking only slightly less woebegone than me, with another large Warden standing over him. Unfortunately, he had been captured immediately, and, because one has to return to one's boat in these situations, they had all just stood around and listened to me shoot.

HEROES AND OUTLAWS

The Wardens, very professional, asked us a few questions, learned that Jack had killed a turkey the day before, and confiscated our guns and licenses. They drove Jack to his house and told him to go get his already cleaned and frozen turkey. His parents were out of town at the time, and he complied. Mr. John was livid about this and several heated telephone conversations ensued between he and the Wardens, which served to fuel an already poor mutual esteem they shared.

Jack was somehow able to get his gun back later, but mine was reported "lost," with no recourse. We were ticketed for trespassing, not tagging, and shooting a hen out of season. Apparently there is no "grey area" about private property rights along the Mississippi River. Also, Tennessee is one of those horrible states that require all big game to be taken to a "check station" within a certain amount of time. It makes no difference that there are no "check stations" open or anywhere nearby wherever you happen to hunt. It is a situation that makes everyone an "outlaw" eventually.

Court was set for a month away. Jack's dad offered to plead our case for us, but because he wasn't a lawyer, and because he didn't get along with these particular Wardens, his services were declined. My dad thought that whatever happened to us would be a good lesson.

After a month of worry, we showed up on the appointed date at Juvenile Court, Memphis, Tennessee, ready to take our licking. Hair combed, coat and tie, and feeling like real scumbugs, we were the only white defendants in the whole building. There were a ton of people there, and a long wait for us, during which our anxiety level skyrocketed. Finally, a large ebony

TAKE ME BACK

bailiff came in and said; "The Judge will see you now." Sheepishly, we shuffled in and stood in front of his Honor.

He was a portly, middle-aged man, with thick glasses and sweaty hair plastered to his head. He looked harried, overworked, and at the moment, puzzled. Looking up from a mountain of paperwork on his desk, he asked us in a high pitched, slow southern drawl, "Ya'll a in heah fo' shootin a tur—key, that right?"

"Yes sir," in unison.

"Was this some—bodies turkey?" he asked.

"No sir, it was wild…and mine was a hen."

Still trying to get a grasp, he asked, "So was it turkey season then?"

"Oh yes sir!" and we proceeded to explain how you can shoot a hen in the fall, but not in the spring, and we really thought we were ok to hunt there, and we didn't mean…"

He held up one hand to stop the rush of words and sat rubbing his temples for a moment before saying, "Listen, I got five boys in the next room on a rape charge, and ya'll in heah for a damn turkey? Get out o' heah and don't ya'll neva come back!"

We never did.

Mallard Hole

In central Arkansas, between the St. Francis and Mississippi rivers, there is a bayou called "Blackfish." This bayou meanders through a land basically flat as a pancake. Heavy clay soils predominate in this once alluvial region and rice is the predominant crop. It is farm country, end to end, and the major watersheds are either channelized or leveed.

It was not always so. The first eyewitness references that I can find for the area are from Freidrick Gerstacker. He was an adventurous young German that traveled and wrote books about the "new world" beginning in the late 1830's. This intrepid twenty-one year old landed in New York and walked all over the eastern United States, for several years, hunting as he went. His first book "Rambling and Hunting in the United States of North America" received great acclaim and he went on to write several more.

Upon reading this book, it occurred to me that Freidrick and I have something in common. Sure, we both love the outdoors (though Freidrick was a lot tougher than I) but we both think this area around Blackfish is special. In those days he would shoot deer, turkey, and waterfowl, around Blackfish for a while, walk over to Little Rock to spot light some deer at a salt lick (he used a fire built on a platform for light)– on the way crawling into a few holes to shoot hibernating bears with some Indian buddies, swing by the Bayou De View prairie region for a buffalo hunt, and then head back to Blackfish to start the whole process over again. He thought that of all the places he went, and there were many, the shooting was best around Blackfish.

In this day and time, the ecology has changed. No more does the vast unbroken forest extend from the Mississippi River westward to the plains and prairies. Clearing, precision leveling, and maximizing returns are the order of the day. Wild turkey no longer abound, except in isolated large-tract woodlands. The deer, though omnipresent and adaptable, can only be a slight fraction of what he saw.

As with most ecosystems, a void is quickly filled by another species. Monoculture rice, alligator-clay soil, and lots of wintertime rainfall make this area "THE" wintering ground for North America's Mississippi and Central flyway waterfowl. The perfect combination of food, topography, latitude, and longitude, funnels the birds in, and unless "froze up," they will stay there for the winter. Even when pushed out by a freeze, they return on the heels of the thaw.

One of the first hunting clubs in the region was situated at Blackfish Lake. According to the historic work "The Golden Age of Hunting," by Wayne Capooth, it was called the "Blackfish Lake Gunning and Trolling Club." Fed by sportsmen out of Memphis, the club had a rocky history due to personal feuds between members and locals, but the hunting was reported to have been excellent.

My own fascination with this area began in the 1970's. My good friend and neighbor, Robert Weaver, a young teenager at the time, was an avid hunter and his dad had just bought some land in the area as an investment. Though the property was not noted as a waterfowl "Mecca" at that time, the previous owner had told Mr. Weaver about the abundance of ducks on the farm whenever there was a "big rain." Apparently, the farm was fairly low, and all previous efforts had been directed at keeping water off the place. Being a visionary type of land owner/waterfowl hunter, Mr. Weaver then built a network of ditches with pipes and gates to hold water on the place and called the whole project "Twin Ridge Farm."

The lowest portion of the farm contains a field of about a hundred acres. In the center of this field grows a stand of variously aged willows. The clump is somewhat star shaped, and resembles an island, which it is not. It is actually just a spot that is even lower than the rest of the field, therefore making it impossible to farm in the spring because it holds water well into summer. Mr. Weaver, Robert, and their farmer, Thomas Couples, decided to build a duck blind in these trees. The blind was just a two-by-four platform with no brush, but the first time it was hunted the ducks swarmed in like bees. This led Mr. Weaver to proclaim a name for the spot, which has endured to this day, some thirty-eight years later. The name given was "Mallard Hole," and over time it became legendary.

The next year the blind was rebuilt to more grandiose dimensions. Mr. Ted Jenestead, a cotton mill buyer from Henderson, North Carolina, was enlisted to oversee construction while Robert and I were "volunteered" to provide unskilled labor. Mr. Jenestead would drink a half-gallon of Jack Daniels, straight out of the bottle, and smoke three packs of cigarettes a day during construction, and it was said that he never missed a nail. His work was phenomenal. The new Mallard Hole blind had an L-shaped shooting porch, sixteen feet on the short side and twenty feet on the other, with trees growing up through the floor. Cleverly hidden behind the long arm was a boat hide, big enough for two boats, and a warming room complete with gas stove, smoked glass windows, and cooking gear. Running Southeast, off the back of the blind, ran a walkway to a privy, and then a continuance for another thirty yards or so to another smaller shooting platform on the backside of the clump of trees. It was Swiss Family Weaver through and through.

The first time they hunted the new Mallard Hole blind I was not there but the stories they told were unbelievable– mallards by the hundreds, hovering over the decoys again and again; wood ducks in a constant tornado that never quit; many, many, other species observed and occasionally shot. They were picky. They could afford to be. Mr. Weaver wouldn't let anyone shoot "woodies" (a common old-school mentality) and most of the effort was on mallard drakes. They did shoot an albino mallard and a crossbreed. They even shot a snow goose, at the time unheard of, but nowdays quite common. They were bad..., terrible even. I was so jealous.

The next weekend I was there. It was just like they had said. Flights of mallards would come from the north, following the bayou, in waves. Mr. Weaver, Robert, and I, would highball on the old black "Olt" calls, and they would peal out like fighter jets, circle once or twice, and come right in. It was glorious, and it made all of us feel like world champion duck callers.

Mr. Weaver had four clients from his cotton business with him that day. About ten o'clock they decided to go back to the clubhouse that Mr. Weaver had built, for some refreshment. We had two boats and so Robert and I elected to stay in the blind. Actually, we were thrilled to get rid of the "old guys" and get down to some serious shooting. You see, up until that time we had been engaged as constant call-and-retrievers. Every time we would be, either coming back in the boat, or wading back with ducks, they shot some more.

Anyway, we did our shooting and then around noon, the flight ceased. We were debating whether to go back, or not, when the other boat was heard approaching. A long ditch used for boat travel passes by the mallard hole field with a turn-in, right in front of the blind. Five big men all bundled up but with no waders on, came into view and turned in the opening. Each of them held a large Styrofoam cup which seemed to glow in the pale winter sun. They were laughing and talking, having a good time. Robert commented that the boat was way-overloaded up front, but that they didn't seem to care. I started moving our ducks off the benches, making room, when suddenly Robert fell to the floor of the blind, laughing. Glancing out front, the cause became immediately apparent. Standing in the middle of the field, in three feet of water, were the five men, holding the five cups over their heads as if they were priceless, and Mr. Weaver yelling—"Robert...Robert... come get me!!" The boat and motor were completely invisible... and nobody spilled a drop!

I hunted with the Weavers many times over the next few years and stayed in their lodge quite often. Mr. Weaver usually had business guests on weekends, and Robert and I were allowed to tag along as boat drivers and bird cleaners. We also did a lot of shooting—well worth it for us. Those were flamboyant groups, as I remember, and necessitated a special kind of leadership from their host. For instance, Mr. Weaver, after a bad experience or two, put a sign on the wall right by the front entryway that read, "you are welcome to bring your duck call, but please, place the reed in here" followed by an arrow pointing down to a cup. I think he meant it. He also kept dozens of cases of shells for his clients to shoot. The load was a federal High-Power 1¼oz #6. I tried them a few times, and a more ineffective load has never been made. It was about like throwing salt at them. Neither I, nor Robert, would use them—and they were free! Nash Buckingham once wrote, "Never send a boy to do a man's job." He was talking about waterfowl guns at the time, but let me add this, "Never was great work done by a man unfed."

Other blinds were built, and they were good on certain days and certain winds, but none ever produced like the Mallard Hole. By the time Robert and I got up to driving age the fame had spread. Mr. Weaver, about as kind-hearted and sociable as anyone I've ever met, gave many an open invitation to "come and hunt anytime." Most just showed up at hunting time, not realizing the year around preparation that went into a first class duck set up.

It came to pass that fame was not always desirable. It appeared that Mr. Weaver did not own the farm independently. There were partners involved, and they wanted to ration the shooting. In his defense, all development costs including ditching, levees, pipes, pumping, blind building, maintenance, and house construction had been born by him, alone, but fame was about to do him in. I don't know what verbal agreements had been made over time, obviously something, but no matter now, the farm was to be split—at least for hunting rights.

They divided the farm into two blocks, and the two groups were to switch at mid season. The blocks were basically: A) Mallard Hole B) The rest of the farm.

The "other" group didn't have a lot of experience in the duck hunting line, and so they enlisted the help of renowned Memphis duck hunter, John Stokes, to set up their blinds and call for them. This was tough for me because John's son, Jack, had been my best friend from nursery school up. There was so much ill will involved, that one could not, in good conscience, hunt with the other team. There is the old saying that you have to "dance with the one what brung ya," so that's where I stayed. The Weaver clan had been too good to me for too long.

The most difficult thing in the world for a duck hunter is to be "almost in the spot." We tried everything;

super hidden blinds, hundreds of decoys—sometimes crowding right up to the line. No matter what we did, including putting tin-foil on top of the Mallard Hole blind (applied at night), the ducks just poured in there. We called ourselves hoarse, wore our hands out pulling jerk-strings, and Mallard Hole would get the ducks nine times out of ten.

This trading back and forth went on for several years until the partnership, due to financial difficulty, decided to sell the farm.

A new buyer, Harry Phillips, quickly appeared and put together a club. This well healed group spared no expense to have the finest duck shooting around— and they got it. John Stokes, and eventually his son Jack, were members, and I continued to get to hunt the farm with them, and a clear conscience.

The new club had rules, and a draw for blinds, necessary evils when there are several equal-share owners. My usual invite was from Jack. Early on, as a member's son, he could hunt but not participate in the draw. Consequently, we never got Mallard Hole. If there were a lot of ducks around it didn't make much difference- we could get a limit easily. But if things were slow, our usual "modus operindi" was to set up somewhere near Mallard Hole, listen to the shooting, and when they were done, dash in there and get our limits. I don't know how many times we did this— getting in there at ten, eleven, or even twelve o-clock (club rules forbade shooting after one p.m.) and having a fabulous hunt—dozens of times, at least.

The Phillips group called the club "Blackfish Bayou Hunting Club," or "Blackfish" for short. As the years progressed this group bought in all memberships that came up for sale until in 2008, during the severe financial crisis, a membership was offered to me, which I bought.

Henry Morgan, club "president," or manager at the time, told me that it was time to rebuild the Mallard Hole blind and "did I have any input?" Little did he know how deep an attachment and long a history I had with the old one which had been raised, lowered, patched, and scabbed onto, a hundred times by ten different architects. I was his man; I wanted to help.

We planned and plotted, got input from the other members, and set the play in motion. Because it was a difficult place to get to, and work in, I didn't trust a carpenter to do it properly, so I took on the job of actual construction personally.

Survey of the site showed seven or eight essential trees were missing. Close inspection lead to the theory that they had all died a violent death— by gunfire, or lead poisoning. Probing around in the mud beneath where the old blind had stood for so many years were rare and ancient treasures. Sunglasses, pocketknives, flashlights— four decades worth, and some of it I remembered. When a posthole was dug, we were still in almost solid shotgun shell hulls at two and a half feet below the surface. This kind of place is a poster for the pro- steel shot lobby.

I couldn't be sure of having enough cover in that spot for the new blind to work like the old one had. Being "the new kid on the block," at least in this group, change was a risky proposition, but there seemed to be no other way around it. During the previous season,

Henry and I had sat in the boat in various nearby locations, just to see how the ducks worked with respect to the current standing tree pattern. We both were worried about the lack of cover in the old spot and identified a likely replacement position. About forty yards to the southwest there was a dense enough stand of growing timber to make it work and it was decided to give it a try.

The membership's shooting habits are different now than they were when the original blind was built. Nowadays, no one shoots over the limit, or stays out all day, and a cook is employed at the lodge, so a warming/cooking room is obsolete. Another big difference has been the popularity of the Go-Devil type motors, specifically the surface drive models. There is no better way to get around in dense vegetation and shallow water, but they don't back up easily. A drive-through boat hide is called for, and this negates the possibility of other structures behind the blind without making things complicated.

I settled on a thirty-foot straight-line platform, facing in the same direction, nearly, as the old blind, two roomy dog platforms, multiple benches at different heights, and multiple trees growing up through the floor throughout. The boat hide is drive-through, with a low level step-out for low water conditions. Painted and brushed, if one remains still, even the hard hunted ducks of today come right in. Gone are the days when large groups, fifty to a hundred mallards, would commit and come in at one time, but that seems to be the way of the world. Now, if a big group gives you a look, three or four come in, and you just hope there is a drake in the bunch.

We still hunt the blind every day of the season, or nearly so. It is still the best spot that I have ever hunted, day-in and day-out. Sometimes, when I am there alone, I think of Mr. Jenestead, and how much care and attention he put into the original blind, these nearly forty years past, and then I think of all the joy and memories so many of us have derived from his handiwork. How many "first" ducks? How many red-letter days? It is with a jolt that I realize that he was about my age when he built the original. Who will be here in another forty? What great memories will be made between now and then?

Whoever they are, if they can get in here on something of a south wind, and have a few really good companions to share the experience, they are probably going to think this is the best danged duck blind in the world. It would make us feel proud, Mr. Ted and I, if we are watching from above.

Mr. Ted and Robert Weaver, circa 1972

Mr. Bobby Weaver, proud of the days kill at Mallard Hole with Robert and the author- circa 1973.

Robert and his grandfather, looking out from the old Mallard Hole blind.

Bait

The mourning dove, Zenaida Mecroura, is America's gamebird. Though classified as "migratory" under the Migratory Bird Treaty Act, they actually nest in every state in the union. North Dakota has the second largest breeding population (behind Texas), and I have seen pairs that were successful in raising two broods, back to back, on my porch in that state. Warmer areas with longer growing seasons have even higher success rates, sometimes up to six broods in a year. The young are called squabs and they are raised two at a time. Their growth rate is phenomenal. One can sneak up and peak at a nest, every day, and easily tell a difference from the last look. The whole process, from egg to fledging, only takes about four weeks with both parents helping, and then they start over. It is estimated that the North American population comes in at about four hundred seventy-five million birds and annual mortality clocks in at about sixty percent. Hunters take around fifty-five million a year and mother nature another two hundred and thirty million. As you can see, shooting is not a limiting factor of the population. A Mississippi state wildlife biologist once told me that the limit could be set at one hundred and it would have no detrimental effect on the population, but license sales would decline because most people would be unable to "get the limit."

I am not an advocate of one hundred bird limits. Fifteen is a nice shoot, and provides ample table fare. My problem is with other regulations. Particularly, baiting regulations.

The federal government, in its infinite wisdom, has decreed that doves may not be shot over bait. The fact that if you don't have bait of some sort then no doves will be shot at all is apparently of no consequence. One may grow sunflowers, mow them down, and shoot doves over them. You may NOT buy sunflowers, spread them on the ground, and shoot doves over them. The same goes for wheat, milo, corn etc. Let us examine this scenario for a moment.

Take a typical southern "dove field" of twenty acres. To plant and grow a crop of sunflowers will cost you somewhere in the vicinity of $250/acre for a grand total of $5,000. If you did a good job, you will end up with twenty acres of stubble and bare dirt with about 30,000 pounds of sunflower seeds on the ground. Lots of doves can feed there and everything is just fine, until it rains. After two or three days of wet weather and high temperatures, everything is either sprouted or rotten—game over.

The same field could be baited for far less money, and have a lot longer lifespan. One can spread 50 lbs/

acre of sunflowers (or whatever is inexpensive) for a fraction of the cost, and reapply as needed. The birds get a steady food supply, ammo sales go up, and more people are attracted to the sport. The point is that there is no difference in the two fields, other than cost and longevity— where is the wisdom in that?

Before you go out and bait your next field, first read up on the regulations. The Migratory Bird Treaty Reform Act of 1998 states that it is unlawful to hunt doves over bait "if one knows or reasonably should know" that bait is present. Talk about rigging things in the governments favor! Furthermore, it states that fines of up to $100K for individuals, and $200K for organizations, with up to one year in prison, or both, may be levied. I don't know about you, but to me this seems a little harsh.

I would consider putting out a little bird seed and shooting a few doves over it with family and friends about as evil as setting my cruise control at sixty-eight in a sixty-five miles per hour zone—on a long drive with no cities around! There is a big push in the US right now to reign in our federal government. Tea party activists are everywhere calling for less frivolous government and obtuse regulation. Maybe we should start here.

I do not bait for doves. When CNN runs a documentary on the "Bad Baiting Laws," and congress calls an emergency session to set everything back right, I will. But until that time I'll just have to remember what it used to be like, in the bad-old days... until I got caught.

Collegiate endeavors had come to pass, and with them, a general up rooting of the normal yearly schedule. Dove shooting, a solemn and sacrosanct yearly tradition, was in danger and needed desperate measures. I called up Ken Flowers, an expert in these forays, and we cooked up a plan. Ken was living in Knoxville, Tennessee and I in Starkville, Mississippi and so we located our field somewhat between us, in Germantown, Tennessee and enlisted his dad as the silent financial backer. I was to get the ground disked up, nice and clean, and Ken was to get some wheat, and plant it nice and even, over the field. We each accomplished our respective tasks, and the very next week, when I was able to visit the field, we were already loaded up with doves. I called Ken up to tell him about it and let him know my fear that they were probably going to eat it out before the season— maybe we should add just a little more, just to be safe? He agreed, and we decided that I would do it because I was a little closer.

Now, college can be a busy time, socially if for no other reason, and the only time I could get it done was at night. I enlisted Robert Weaver, another expert in the field, to ride on the back tailgate of my Blazer and carefully spread the wheat far and wide as I plied a course in the original tracks of the first planting. Robert may have been drinking beer, but his capacity at that time was legendary, and thus he had my complete confidence in a professional job.

Reports soon came in of even vaster numbers of birds. Now, there was a veritable grey cloud in the air all afternoon and five or six constant flight lanes approaching like spokes of a wheel.

I got nervous. Could Robert get some help and freshen up the field? I couldn't make it back that week.

Be careful! No new tracks, and make sure it is spread evenly! Meanwhile, miscommunication with Ken; He had organized his own night-time operation, and had replanted the entire field, and added a little rock salt— just to give it a little boost.

Clearly we were treading on thin ice. A halt was called to all future operations and we settled down to wait, and hope that the doves could eat all the excess grain and glitter before the season opened.

Our field was small, a mile and a half from a paved road, and behind a locked gate. Surely we wouldn't attract any attention.

"The guilty flee when no man pursueth" came to mind when we did not hunt it on opening weekend. We were nervous because the "planting" operation, which invariably went on in the dark, and at the back of the truck, had not been done in as conscientious a manner as had been envisioned. Wheat had been poured out in long, wavy, curves, between the tire tracks, which ran in all directions. There was green wheat coming up, in dense, squiggly lines, and newer, golden lines, poured on top, and in all directions. Add to that the twinkle and flash of rock salt, which gave it the air of a South African diamond mine. The intricate patterns and colors were probably noticeable from passing commercial jetliners, at cruising altitude.

Ah, but the birds were there. It was decided to risk it. A quick shoot Labor Day, then everyone could flee back to school.

Only the people involved, monetarily or physically, were invited. Robert Shy, Robert Weaver, and I, pulled up to the field and the Flowers family was already shooting. Doves circled like angry bees at a kicked-over hive. New flocks poured in from all directions to add to the confusion. It was with shaking hands that shells were dumped out of boxes and into vests and guns snatched out of cases. We shot our guns blister-hot for about forty-five minutes, and then, with nearly simultaneous mutual consent, we decided to get out... now. Each of us had a feeling that something was not right. We had seen no one, there were no tracks, but some of the aircraft flying about looked suspicious. Probably nothing to worry about; there were always planes and helicopters in that area; anyway, we had all had plenty of shooting and did not wish to push our luck.

The two Roberts and I left first, and when within sight of the road we stopped to reconnoiter from the top of the Wagoneer. Tall corn made it difficult to see, but it appeared that a uniformed person was at the gate. Weaver and I were both eighteen, and could be tried as adults, so we decided to negate that possibility by leaving on foot. Mr. Shy was to pick us up at an old barn, about a mile away and across an ocean of standing corn, whenever he could. As soon as this plan was made, a couple of green-clad figures came into view, sprinting our way down the fence line. Weaver threw his keys in the truck window and said, "It's your truck now Shy," and vaulted the fence. I followed, and as soon as we were out of sight, ditched birds, guns, and started running.

It must have been one hundred and thirty degrees Fahrenheit in the corn and not a breath of wind. An earlier noticed helicopter began making low passes over the field and an airplane began circling higher up. Motion attracts the eye, and we made our way by cowering motionless as the chopper's blades thrashed the corn stalks, and then sprinting, when plane and chopper were facing away. Eventually we reached a position from which we could watch the barn lot from concealment. A half hour passed as we sweated away on the ground. Soon, a car could be heard on the gravel of the barn lot, and then a door opened and closed. Surely it was way too early for Robert to pick us up? Ever so slowly, we inched our heads above the weeds to take a look.

"FREEZE, put your hands in the air!" We spun around and were amazed to see a game warden, pistol drawn, covered in sweat and gasping for breath, not ten yards away. The poor man then said- "Please, don't run anymore! I think I'm having a heart attack!" He wasn't kidding, past middle aged, and over weight, the cornfield had about done him in. We took him over to the horse barn, where cold water ran from a pipe into a large trough. After a few minutes of cool down he quit gasping and could speak on his walky-talky.

It was a sheepish looking group back at the field, and our rejoining didn't add much levity. The only people having any fun were the eight federal agents who had put so much time and effort into our capture. They showed us aerial photographs, taken over weeks, which documented our "planting" activities. They had been hiding around the field for three days, waiting for us to show. Pictures of us shooting had been taken and comments were made about various hits and misses and how close we had been to hidden watchers at times. One of the younger wardens, with a big telephoto lens, said that "that boy in the green T-shirt" (Robert Weaver) was the best shot he had ever seen, "went twenty-nine straight and not picking easy shots either!" Sometimes, even compliments can be unwelcome.

Eventually, the party started to wind down, citations were issued, and those needing to head back to various universities did so.

The local newspaper listed all the various busts and the accompanying fines accrued during the first dove season. There were quite a few, as I remember, but right at the top, was ours. Numbers one and two, at $750 each and a long list of offenses was yours truly, and Robert Weaver. I always wanted to be number one in the state at something.

As a side note, about a week after the hunt I received a crank call from John Stokes pretending to be a federal judge and demanding my presence in court immediately. He scared about a year off my life span, and some day I'm going to get even. A further aside, and final chapter to this story, came about a year later. Apparently the local wardens had also been involved in our bust and Mr. John happened to run into one around town. The two men were not friends, theirs was even a somewhat adversarial relationship, and the warden commented that it was too bad John had not been present at the "big shoot." Mr. John, thinking this a rather rude thing to say, just looked at him for a slow moment, and then said, "I was."

Indiana Ray

It had been a dry fall, and thereby a tough season, for the roving public-land duck hunter set. Even with the absence of water, and therefore waterfowl, the sun still rose everyday and the calendar would not pause, and wait for better conditions. Duck season was slipping away.

High school, that great deterrent to the proper fulfillment of one's shooting ambitions, had paused for the Christmas break, and we, Jack and I, were going hard.

Our options were limited. Neither the Cash River, nor the White, or any of their tributaries, held ducks except when flooded. Contrary to the writings of old, the Mississippi River gets almost no duck usage when low. Ducks don't even stay in an area unless ample feeding, resting, and escape areas can be easily accessed. The "big clubs," with their pumped up woods and rice fields, were doing well, but we weren't in one.

Our best option had been the "Broad Waters" of the massive St. Francis Sunken Lands.

This area of Northeast Arkansas called the "Sunken Lands" came into being during the New Madrid earthquakes of 1811 and 1812. The same quakes that created famous Reelfoot Lake also brought a thirty-mile long stretch along the St. Francis River to a lower elevation. Early accounts tell of tall trees having their tops barely above water level when it was over. This can easily be confirmed by trying to drive a boat down this river during low water levels. I have broken many a shear pin and propeller while learning the safe channels. At one point, down below the old Hatchie Coon club and before you get to the siphon tubes, the river gets wide and shallow, like a giant lake maybe a mile wide, depending on water levels, and several miles long, dotted with cypress trees—some in clumps, others alone. Many of these trees are very old, and were probably already established within the bottomland forest before the quake. Now, all the hardwood is dead and gone (except the stumps), and the cypress carry on in a world flooded year-round.

This area is what locals call "The Broad Waters," and it is a very unusual place. Ducks work into this area from the absolute stratosphere. Unfortunately, it is no secret. The entire area is covered in duck blinds; hardly a lone tree that does not have a floating blind attached to it. Many, many, of the blinds have vast "big water" decoy spreads, and are hunted every day of the season. Competition is keen; multiple duck callers/blind; lots of highballing and minute attention to decoy placement with prompt adjustments for wind are the norm. It is not unusual for a dozen blinds, with hundreds of decoys each, to be calling at the same ducks. Herein, I believe, lies the key to the success of the place. It must look, and sound, like a federal wildlife refuge to migrating flights.

And into this mêlée we proposed to go. Our modus operandi, thus far, had been to arrive at daylight; ride around a bit and see where the ducks were working that day; find an unused blind near the action- hopefully with decoys; adjust the spread, fix the tangles etc, and get ready for the ten to two flight—usually the most productive time of the day.

This day was to be different. The day before we had found an unused blind, in a good place, that had not even been brushed for the year. Tired of being "bumped" from other people's blinds, we were going to "take over" this unused jewel. To do so required a lot of work. We had cut brush the afternoon before and stacked it on the bank. We had re-strung and re-patched, every decoy that we could beg, borrow, or steal. Finally, we had allocated four hours, before shooting time, to get set up. We were at the ramp putting our boat in at two o-clock in the morning.

My newest acquisition, a well broke-in thirty-five horse Johnson outboard motor, was having its debut that day. Bought for its price, rather than any particular quality it might have possessed, it was expected to whisk our fourteen-foot johnboat speedily about our chores. It was with great pride of ownership and long awaited anticipation that it was brought proudly from its resting cradle in the back of the truck. Having screwed the monster to the transom, hooked up fuel line, primed, opened the vent and pulled the choke out, I said a small prayer of thanks as my left hand slowly caressed the powerful machine. Jack began loading sacks of decoys for the first trip out as my right hand fingers entwined about the black rubber end of the pull cord. My left hand fingers encircled those, and I set my left leg for a mighty pull.

Forty minutes later, after two, ten-minute shifts apiece, of the hardest pulling either of us had ever encountered, the beast just sat there and looked at us. Frost had formed on all of our equipment, but not us, we were stripped down to T-shirts, and panting. About then, a dim glow appeared on the canal... a good ways off... and getting closer.

Slowly, and almost silently, a pointed duck boat came ghosting into view, its bow light throwing out feeble rays into the mists hanging low over the water. A voice, kindly and cheerful, incongruous with the apparition, spoke out. "Mornin," it said, "Having motor trouble?" With sweat running down our faces, and between pants, we asserted the accuracy of the statement. "Would ya'll like some coffee?" it said.

"No, thank you, we're fine, but thanks anyway, just need to get this new motor started."

Then the voice said, "I'm Ray, and I'll be back by here in about fifteen minutes to check on you. I've got an extra boat if you need one."

No-no, we would be fine, we were sure it would start soon, but thanks very much, we'll see you out there.

The fifteen minutes passed, another three shifts pulling, and we were whipped.

True to his word, Ray ghosted silently back into view in a different boat, a bigger square front version with a gleaming, purring, brand new outboard on the back. The motor barely made a sound as it idled smoothly away, a perfect stream of water shooting out the back as we stared, enviously. "Why don't ya'll hop in with me?" he said. We couldn't possibly, no, no, we wouldn't want to intrude, no thanks, we'll be fine etc… "I'm by myself, nobody to hunt with, come on if you want to," he said.

"Well…uhm.. that might be… where are you going?" I asked.

"I've got four of the best blinds on the Broadwaters, I'm headed to round pond today, I'm thinking."

Trying to be helpful I ventured, "Do you need any decoys?"

His reply was matter of fact "No, I've got five hundred or so out at each blind, and they look perty good." We looked at each other, Jack and I, skepticism oozing from every pore. This was too good to be true, who was this guy? Why was he by himself? What was he doing up so early? What the heck, we loaded our guns and shell buckets into his boat and shoved off.

Jack whispered, "Wonder where we're going at three am?" "Me too," I said, "Like being early, but he said the decoys were already out!"

From the back of the boat, and over the now humming outboard, Ray told us "There's a thermos of hot chocolate and mugs under your seat, and bacon an egg sandwiches!"

Who was this guy? We pondered that question as we were sped smoothly down the canal, munching sandwiches and drinking hot chocolate.

Ray never hit a stob, and never slowed down, on the fifteen-minute run to round pond. Just as he had said, there were at least five hundred decoys out, and they were immaculate. The blind was a "shooters blind," with elevated platforms to step up on and have three hundred and sixty degree's of visibility and swing. The brushing looked great, and it was now half past three o'clock of a beautiful, starry, night.

As we sat and listened to the chatter and feint whistling wings of occasional passing flights, invisible, in the nighttime sky, Ray produced more groceries, including brownies, and hot chocolate mixed with coffee. He seemed to have an inexhaustible supply. With open candor and a genuine friendliness, he began to tell us a little bit about himself. He was from Indiana, a plumber, and had somehow married a local "river rat's" daughter. His passion was, and always had been, duck hunting, and he worked hard nine months out of the year, and then came down here for duck season, the entire season, and hunted all day every day. "Would you like another sandwich?"

By this time, we were getting quite full, and actually declined, probably a first for either of us. With nothing to do for the next three hours before daylight, Jack and I started calling ducks. Ray was amazed, "Wow, you guys are good! Never got the hang of it myself. Do ya'll ever shoot the 'black ball'?" Before we could respond, a big flight of mallards that had been circling, chose that moment to give a low pass and banked right in to the front of the blind. There must have been fifty or more in the bunch and they all committed at once. Jack and I kept up the small talk, and walked them right across the decoys, and up close, admiring their silhouettes. Quite unexpectedly, the front of the blind erupted in streaks of fire and thunderous noise. Six times, and right into the middle of the flock. As Ray was frantically reloading his gun, and maintaining a steady barrage at the escaping cripples, noticed only by the "V's" they made on the water reflected in the starlight, he said, "How come ya'll didn't shoot?"

We were too dumbfounded to answer right away, as Ray hopped into the boat and motored around, sending occasional long stabs of fire out across the water. What had we gotten ourselves into? Here we were, in the middle of the most heavily hunted piece of public water in the country, in somebody we didn't know's boat, who was making noise like WWII, at a quarter to four in the morning. More shots and flames echoed across the water as Ray rounded up the last few cripples, shooting in front of the "V's."

Finally, our generous host returned, "Would ya'll like any more coffee? How come you didn't shoot? Don't you know how to hit the black ball?" OH..., so that's what he meant...

Inspection revealed that Ray carried three guns with him. A Browning 2000 auto, plug in. An Ithaca Mag 10, plug in, and a single shot 12 gauge "Long Tom" with a thirty-six inch barrel, in the boat for cripples. Apparently, Ray's scruples did not allow him to shoot an unplugged gun. His technique was to shoot the Browning first, followed by the Mag 10, for get-aways, and early cripple shots, and the long Tom stayed in the boat, loaded and ready. It was effective.

Sometimes young people can be influenced by the people they come in contact with; and Ray assured us that nobody was up yet and therefore we were perfectly safe. On the next bunch our shots joined the barrage, and it was quite a volley because we had taken our plugs out to sort of "even things up." Why not? We were in an unusual situation.

By the time the first outboard motor could be heard on any part of the river, and before the first truck came to back down on the heavily used public ramp, Ray had delivered us back to our truck with a big pile of mallards. He asked us to come hunt with him anytime, any day of the season, as he pulled away from the landing, whistling, and just happy to be looking forward to another fine day of duck hunting.

Thus began our association with "Indiana Ray" as we called him, and many a fine shoot it led to for several years thereafter. Though we never participated in another "black ball" shoot, (We did have a few scruples, even then)– Ray always welcomed us when we would just "show up" during the day. He always had plenty of food, a trademark of his, and he was always where the ducks wanted to be. About the third year after our first meeting, Ray stopped coming. We made some inquiries with the locals, but never found out what happened to him. Ray was an enigma, in more ways than one.

Old Ways

I like the old ways. Sometimes colder, often wetter, but always accompanied by golden memories of heroic action and steely resolve, where pain and discomfort did not exist. Memories are that way. Time sooths and polishes any bumps or burrs that might protrude from a good one. In my oldest memories my shoes always fit, I could run forever, and I was never hungry. These are lies, I know, but they are my memories, darnit, and I'll polish as much as I want.

Early memories are where the old ways are kept. That could be why they are always so smooth and comfortable. The experiences each of us has are quite different in substance, but I am betting they are very similar in "feel." It's a comfort zone mechanism that is endemic to our species and makes us prefer one thing over another.

For instance, I like old guns. Guns with blueing on them and wooden stocks. Guns that have been places and done things, and still can. As a youngster, I didn't see many automatics. An occasional Remington 1100, which was the jaminist gun ever made, and was usually carried only by people who... how would you put it... didn't get out very often, and the Browning A-5's, which had a cult following but still exhibited their fair share of problems, but that was about it. I like double barrels, or pumps, and the simpler the mechanism the better. To me, the measure of a gun can be taken in two ways, and they are both equally important: first, how it shoots; if you can't hit with it you won't like it; second is dependability. Day in and day out, in all weather, it has to work, clean or dirty. I'm not saying you can forget maintenance, but a day or so missed shouldn't make much difference.

Go to any dove shoot nowadays, or get in any duck blind, or look on the rack in any store, and all you see are automatics- snazzy camo-colored jobs with futuristic "style" features that swap out in case you decide to take it into combat. Most of them weigh about six and a half pounds and claim "recoil reduction systems." I don't care how many springs and pistons are added to these already complicated machines, if you shoot three and a half inch magnums out of them you are going to get stomped. Old guns have metal in them, and metal means weight. Weight means smoother shooting with bigger loads—it's just physics.

A few seasons back we had paper-hulled shotgun shells. I have fond memories of them but not because of how they shot, or functioned in adverse conditions— if you dropped them in the water they swelled up two gauges, and fiber base and cap wads didn't help the pattern any—but because of their smell. Burnt powder wafting from a just fired or recently fired paper hull is a true delight to the senses and if I come across an old case somewhere I'm going to buy it just to smell one every once in a while.

The old ways included getting wet all the time. Water, back in the day, was not as harsh as now. While temperatures in my memory were always colder than modern day, the water itself was somehow gentler and less inclined to ruin one's day. I'm not sure how the element has changed over time, but it has, I'm sure of it.

Clothing has changed the most, and not all for the better. Long underwear choices are legion and seem to be mostly about advertising. I've tried most of them but am now married for eternity to cotton and wool, which I believe you will agree, have been around for quite some time. Rainwear and waterproof finishes have spawned whole new industries to keep us dry and sweat-less. Most of them work, for a while, usually a very short while, and then they are trash. Waxed cotton canvas works just as well, and when you detect a leak, rub on some more wax. That's another one from the old school.

I will say that gloves are many-many times warmer than they used to be. Not any more waterproof, just warmer. A new pair of three-hundred gram Thinsulate/Gore-tex gloves will stay waterproof, if at all, for only a very short time, but the warmth they give is amazing. Far better than cotton jersey, or leather over wool lining—and they weren't waterproof either.

Boots have made no progress in my lifetime. Kevlar, speed-laces, micro-bacterial-expelerators, and nano-micron moisture barriers are all just big words designed to make you fork out more money. A solid, well-made plain leather boot, with a large can of mink oil, does everything the new guys claim and does it longer.

I won't say aluminum boats aren't tougher than their older wooden cousins, but they don't have the same feel. Wooden boats are quiet, less tippy, and have a soul. Each one was made individually, by a person, who spent a lot of time doing it, and liked what he was doing. A wooden boat makes a statement about who you are, and what you value. I need to make another one.

Decoys have come a long way lately. Today's models have feather-perfect detail and "photo finishes." They look picture perfect but they don't have a history and nobody is ever going to collect them. Wooden decoys, because of the effort involved in carving them, will always be rare. Looking at some of the oldest ones, you immediately envision market gunning days on big water, punt guns, and Chesapeake Bay Retrievers. When I was young, decoys were mass-produced out of a treated cardboard-like substance. It seems odd, I know, but they actually worked quite well. All I ever saw were mallards, they were fairly durable, and biodegradable to boot. This last fact had to have worked well for the company making them and why they ever switched to plastic I don't know. When I was a kid my dad's club, Hatchie Coon, bought them by the gross every year and I still get a "warm-fuzzy" every time I see one.

The modern duck hunter "breasts" his ducks. Sure it saves time but the skin helps keep the meat moist and the fat underneath is what imparts the flavor that makes duck so good to eat. At my club, we still pick our ducks, and if you try a few on the smoker you won't go back.

The old ways included a lot of work. Often we would scout for several days to find just the right spot and then put an enormous amount of effort into building just the right blind with the perfect decoy spread. When hunting day came we shot hard, usually for the whole day or a good part of it. If everything went well it would be drakes only, to keep our numbers down. The satisfaction that comes from trying really hard, and having it work, is priceless.

Old ways included a level of common courtesy not usually exhibited in today's world. It was rare for anyone to set up near enough to be called competition when duck hunting, unless of course you were on the St. Francis River. That was dog eat dog out there as long as I can remember. On dove shoots, it was considered rude to step in on someone else's flight-lane, even if there was room. Turkey hunters who arrived first on some lonely pre-dawn road were left alone; you should have been there earlier.

Kids were given much latitude. First shots, best places, then as now, but were expected to pull their weight. As they got older, they were expected to take all the tough jobs, without being told to do so, it was considered just part of the training. Manners were noticed also, and if a kid didn't have them he probably didn't get invited back. We all know plenty of kids who have gone far in this world on manners alone.

Many an outdoors man or woman who grew up in my time is alive today. No doubt we all have differing experiences and memories that vary widely. Geographic customs and differing game species across the continent would assure that it be so. But most of them, I'll bet, given the chance, would have to say that they prefer the "old ways," whatever they might be.

Mentors and Ethics

Every sportsman starts his or her career as somewhat of a blank slate. Through experience and observation we learn not only proficiency, but also values, and sometimes, if all the pieces fall into place, a deep and passionate love for all things wild. I have been blessed with many mentors. Not all of them were older, or necessarily wiser, than me. Some had vast experience, others common sense. A few just stood up for what they believed. I'm going to name some of the people that I have learned from, and maybe identify a lesson or two. I hope the reader will be able to see a correlation between this listing and his own life's story. If you do, you are very lucky.

My mom and dad were outdoors people. Not necessarily hunters, but avid and diversified in their outdoors pursuits. Anyone who knew me in adolescent times would tell you that I grew up in a zoo. Pets, both wild and domestic, roamed our house and yard. Emus, iguanas, African tortoises, goats, and pigs, showed up from time to time. Dogs, cats, chickens, and fish, were present in sometimes overwhelming numbers. Horned toads, caymans and snakes, lived in a conservatory abundant with exotic ferns, mosses and orchids. This was because of Mom; she was a collector of wild things.

Most families, when they go to the beach, go to a beach. We went "collecting." Dad loaded the Grinch (Louise, my big sister) and I in the back of the station wagon, Mom up front, pop-up camper behind, and drove down to "Penny Camp" in the Florida keys. We collected shells for an entire week. Some were found on the shoreline but most we dove for or dug up on the mudflats. Apparently this was before restrictions on that sort of thing. Evenings were spent with numerous shell books, Audubon guides, and encyclopedias, in classification. I think I knew the name of every kind of bi-valve or mollusk that grows down there, what it ate, how it lived, and usually how to find it. Most of that collection I still have today, and it is amazing.

On the day before we were to leave Penny Camp, we collected for the aquarium. Dad had set up a saltwater aquarium of several hundred gallons back home. For this we needed live specimens. He sent us out with nets and buckets to collect seaweeds, sponges, corals, fish, and invertebrates. The specimens were then put in trash bags with seawater, inflated by mouth, and tied securely around the top. Just about everything lived, and provided a wonderful microcosm back in Memphis.

Growing up in constant proximity to all this biodiversity one cannot help but learn something about animals and nature—the faithfulness of some dogs, the selfishness of a cat, or the cold, hard, stare of a reptile intent only upon survival. I also learned a good bit about the interaction of species with their environment, and especially, how we are all connected, the balance of nature. Like the species collected, we all live in the same aquarium, and it is a fascinating one. You will be interested to know that the sole survivor in the aquarium, after many years, was the lowly, mindless, blue crab. Take that how you wish.

My uncle and granddad, on the Buckingham side, taught me the mechanics of hunting and fishing. Gun safety, the habits of fish and game, care and maintenance of equipment and how to use it were invaluable lessons, but perhaps the greatest lesson was sportsmanship. These two men epitomized the concept of "gentlemen sportsmen," and did not associate with others who did not. Though I might have strayed from their teachings once or twice, I will always strive to live up to the ideal.

Some of my dad's friends were instrumental, from time to time, in various forms of education. John Austin owned and trained some great Labradors and let me work as a bird boy for the Memphis amateur retriever trials. Stan Jolly took me duck hunting on Tunica Cut-Off, where we would stay from dawn to dark. With him I learned something of patience, and that it is not all about "how many did you get"—we rarely got anything. Another friend of Dad's, whom my uncle nicknamed

"The Great I Am," demonstrated the negative value of boastfulness and unsportsmanlike conduct.

A larger impact was made by John Stokes Jr. Through example, he has taught both his own son and I about camaraderie, hard work, perseverance, and true appreciation of the outdoors and the people we share it with. Without a mean bone in his body, he does everything in life with the same gusto and enjoyment. We should all wish for such energy. I have been at the top of a mountain, which turned out to be the base of the next mountain, looking up into the clouds where a faint Elk bugle had come from, winded and worn out, when John, thirty years my senior, says, "Boys, we don't have a hair on our asses if we don't get on up there," and we went. I have studied the mother-load of ducks with binoculars, a mile out in the middle of a 5,000 acre gumbo mud bean field, with no way to hunt them and not a twig to hide behind, when John would say, "We gotta try!," and we would. It didn't always work, but it was not from lack of effort.

Bobby Weaver owned a farm in Arkansas that he turned into one of the best duck shooting places in North America. During my youth, he was a risk-taker, outgoing and flamboyant in lifestyle, energetic, and genuinely liked people. A great shot, excellent golfer, and good with a duck call, to him it was all about friends, and that's an important lesson.

The people of your own age that you enjoy the outdoors with will always have an impact on one's ethics. Hal Patton showed Jack and I, one day on the Bayou De View, how a true sportsman should act. It's not about how many, it is about going, shooting, killing

MENTORS AND ETHICS

some, laughing, and enjoying the whole experience. Ted O'Brien, who took the time to teach me how to call and hunt turkeys, is an avid outdoorsman of great skill and energy. He has been a quadriplegic now for about twenty years and has never given up. He rules an information empire for hunting and fishing, over the Internet, whereby he keeps up with a vast network of nimrods and can be counted on to know all the latest "scoop." Robert Weaver could teach anyone that you don't have to try so hard to have a good time. Clayton George will always go his own way, and that can be a good thing for anyone to do. Ken Flowers taught me not to worry so much about what other people think, and Jack Stokes, well, Jack and I have learned the same lessons together, over the years. Mainly, that good friends make the good times better, and the bad times not as bad.

I hope you enjoyed this book. It was written by an over-middle-aged-starting-to-get-pudgy guy, with a bad back, who is trying not to farm anymore. I hope it made you remember your own "early years" and the wonder of discovery that we all go through. Good luck and God bless you.

Louise Neely, "The Grinch," my sister, standing on our mobile marine laboratory. "Penny Camp," the Florida Keys 1970.

John W. Stokes Jr. and his companion of many years, Grady, at home in Mallard Hole.

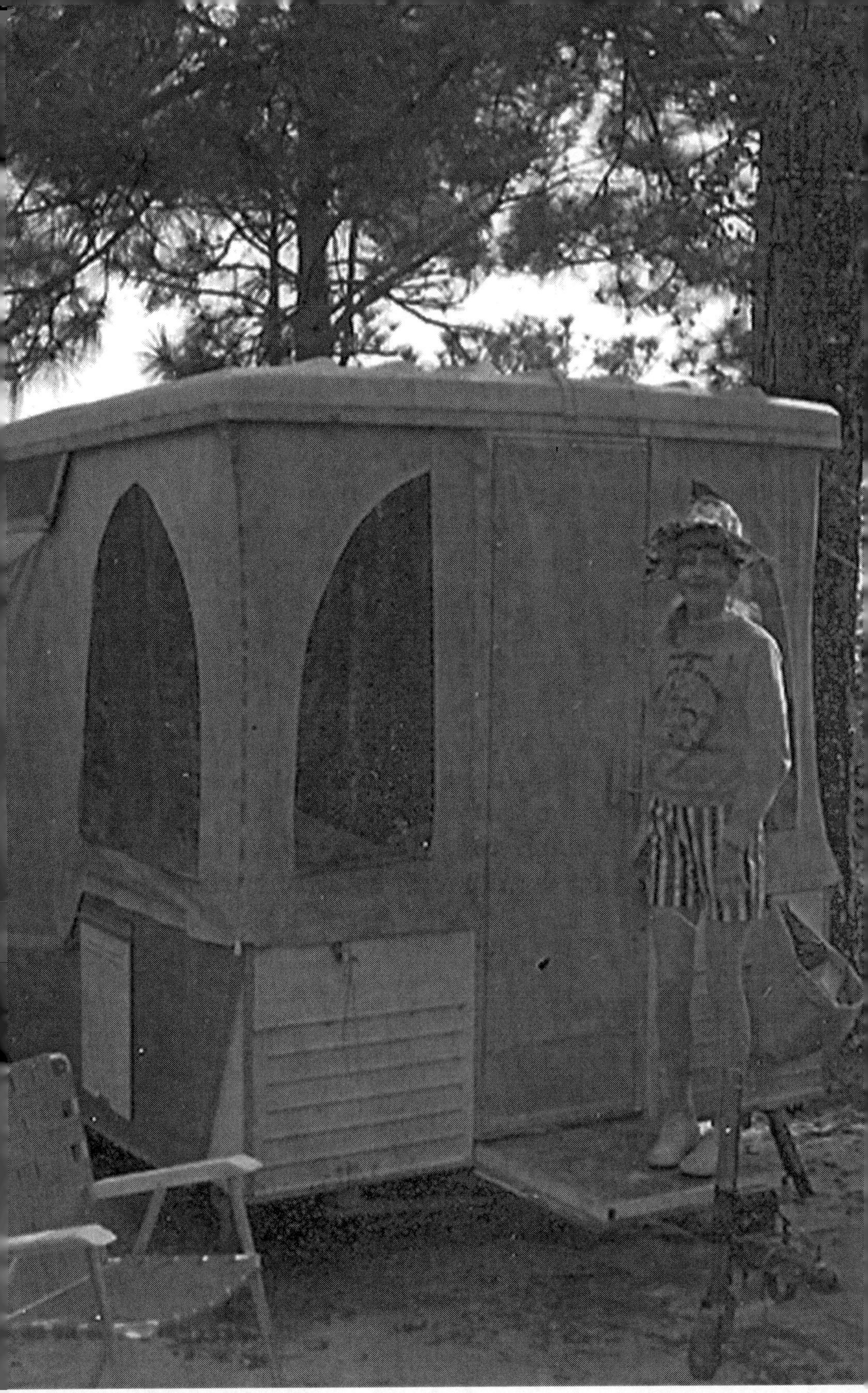